Healing Your Sexual Self

Dr. Janet Geringer Woititz

Health Communications, Inc.
Deerfield Beach, Florida

Library of Congress Cataloging-in-Publication Data

Woititz, Janet Geringer.
     Healing your sexual self / Janet G. Woititz.
        p.   cm.
     Bibliography: p.
     ISBN 1-55874-018-X
     1. Adult child sexual abuse victims.   I. Title.
RC569.5.A28W65   1989   88-32635
616.85'83—dc19   CIP

Published by: Health Communications, Inc.
                3201 S.W. 15th Street
                Deerfield Beach, Florida 33442

Cover Design by Reta Thomas

Dedication

To survivors of abuse
who can use a little help
in their journey toward wholeness.

Acknowledgments

I wish to thank all those who have shared their life experience with me in order to help validate others, and Mel Sandler, M.S.W., and Alice Moore, Ed.D., for their clinical expertise.

— J.G.W.

Contents

*Guilt may be power for the victim,
but tools for living are
the power for the survivor.*

Prologue

This book will discuss breaking the ties caused by too early sexual experience and/or enmeshment. It is about the interference in the process of individuating that one must overcome in order to enter into realistic and healthy relationships — sexual or otherwise. I have no doubt that this can happen. Awareness is the first step. Then you have choices. Acting on the healthy choices is the beginning of a new history, one that will aid you in your recovery from your earlier trauma as you work at healing your sexual self.

A few months ago I had dinner with a friend whom I had not seen in a long time. After we had brought each other up to date, he turned to me and said, "Writing any good books lately?"

"Funny you should ask," I said. "I just happen to be working on a new one. It's about what happens to adults who have been sexually abused or had their sexuality abused as children, and how those experiences play out in their adult lives in ways that may or may not be sexual. It's the most difficult book I've ever written. The material is so emotionally charged that it was months after I had completed the research before I could even begin to put it down on paper."

"Well get with it!" he said. "You just happen to be writing about what I am living, and I want to see how it comes out."

"Tell me."

"I am in a relationship with a wonderful woman. Jeannie is so special I cannot even begin to tell you. I never thought I had a chance, and I want this to work. We have had one major stumbling block since the beginning that doesn't seem to get better. No amount of talking and reassuring has made a difference. She doesn't trust me. The truth is she doesn't trust anybody, but I only care that she doesn't trust me. I give her nothing to be suspicious of, but she still doesn't trust. She used to accuse me of caring more about my mother than I did her, and I bought that for a while, but I stopped being sucked into that one.

"Anyway, just last night I had had it and I yelled at her, 'How can I be in a relationship with someone who doesn't trust me. I love you but I can't stand your constant paranoia. I've had it.' Frankly I was angry enough to walk.

"She broke down and sobbed hysterically. 'Do you think I want to be like this? I hate it as much as you do.' She then told me a story that broke my heart. When she was ten years old her mother remarried. He was a very nice man and very good to her. He told her mother that it would be good for the stepfather-stepdaughter relationship if they had some alone time, and he worked it out so that he would put her to bed and give her a glass of warm milk to help her sleep. This went on for several weeks. He would take her the milk; she would drink it and go to sleep. She would then have recurring dreams that he would come into her room during the night, lift up her nightgown and molest her. She worried about it constantly but believed it was probably a dream and said nothing.

"One day in a highly confidential conversation with her girlfriend Susie, she told Susie about her weird dreams. Susie broke Jeannie's confidence and told her own mother. Susie's mother said that maybe Jeannie was being drugged and to find a way to not drink the milk without his knowing it so she could find out for sure what was going on.

"The following night she pretended to drink the milk while she was in the bathroom but threw it down the toilet. She lay terrified in her bed pretending to be asleep. Sure enough, he came into the room and started to pull down her covers. She bolted out of bed and ran downstairs. She called her friend, and Susie's mom said she had no choice but to tell her mother.

"When she told her mother, her stepfather accused her of lying, and her mother sided with him and called her a little tramp and threatened to send her away if she ever said another word like that to anyone.

"The abuse stopped from then until she left for college. But she was treated like a leper in her own home. Since that time she has been unable to trust anyone.

"She is seeing a good therapist and I have offered to go with her if it would be helpful to her and us. At least now I can be a little more patient."

"Yes, that's precisely what the book is about," I said. "And frankly, you are one of the people I had in mind when I first began thinking about it. I'm not surprised that she threw up your relationship with your mother to you in the argument."

"I'm ahead of you on that one," he said. "A few weeks ago I was sitting with a cousin of mine at a Children of Alcoholics conference in San Francisco," he continued. "My cousin asked me how I was adjusting to my mother's death in light of the covertly incestuous nature of our relationship. I was dumbfounded. 'What are you talking about? What do you mean?'

"She said, 'I'm talking about how amazed I've always been that you became your own person and survived the enmeshment that your mother demanded. You are so much of an individual that I have no understanding of how that could've happened.' In an instant a great many things began to fall into place. Key questions in my life became clear. Answers to questions I'd known the answer to all along took on new meaning.

"I had often said in referring to my mother, 'All she wants of me is my soul. She just wants me to be her image of what I was . . .'

"Since I know many people who tell similar stories, I didn't realize how big this was for her and certainly for me. I had never understood how I could be so individualistic growing up in such a traditional and matriarchal household. My father's input was strictly financial. He was rarely at home, and when he was there, he was off by himself. It became clear that the only way not to be absorbed into my mother was to push out as powerfully as I could. How clear. It makes perfect sense to me now.

"In some aspects of my life this reaction to my mother turned out to be a part of me that I can appreciate. I am pleased that I have had the energy to do the things I believe in in my life.

"Not all the impact was favorable. Although I had speculated about it, I had never fully understood why I was such a natural for an alcoholic marriage. Since there was no alcoholism in my immediate family, there had to be another explanation.

"My mother's desire for me to be connected to her at the hip may be at the core of the matter. If I disagreed or asserted myself, the argument would accelerate. Holding my ground meant she would withdraw her affection. Giving in and apologizing was not the answer either. I had to agree with her thinking. That scrambled me inside and would make me question my own reality. It was certainly better to be compliant.

"That was a perfect setup for co-dependency. Keep friction to a minimum. After all, anything else simply wasn't worth it. And since she was against my marriage — no other woman would have been good enough — I had to deny any problems or hide them in order to maintain my right to my separateness. If I admitted to problems, not only was I wrong in my choice of mate but she was right and her reality was the only choice.

"Since anger meant rejection and withdrawal of affection, I did not understand that I could both love my wife and be outraged at her behavior. This neatly tied the knot. Since I knew I loved her, the negative feelings had to be repressed, explained away or denied.

"Although my mother died this past December and talking about it is part of my need to gain greater understanding of myself, I still feel very disloyal when I do it. She would not approve. Although I would like to believe that I do not seek her approval, I know it would hurt her because she simply could not understand on any level that what is in my best interest has to be defined by me.

"Fortunately, I now know that I can break the tie and still love her."

Introduction

"Why bother reliving the past? It's over and done with, and _____'s dead, so I prefer to forget it and go on."

The question is perfectly valid, and the point of view is understandable. It is true that some of the anxiety will die when whoever abused you dies. You will, for example, no longer have to be frantic at the idea that your child may be left alone in the same room with the offender. You will no longer have to fight back the memories in order to carry on a conversation. If the offender happens to be someone in your immediate family, you will no longer have to feel you are crazy because you still want that person's love even after what he — or she — did to you. You no longer have to promise yourself that you are going to confront the offender once and for all, to have it out in the open. You can give up the pretending game.

Yes — all that is true. But for most adults who have been sexually abused as children, the death of the offender is only a small landmark on the journey of recovery because the experience of sexual abuse affects their daily lives in a variety of ways.

Do you have anxiety about being close? Do you pick partners and lifestyles that are destructive to you? Do you have difficulty combining love and sex? Do you suffer bouts of depression and/or rage that are difficult to explain, or find that even having the explanation doesn't change anything? If your answer to any of these questions is *yes*, you may find this book useful.

Are you able to have an intimate relationship that is healthy both in the bedroom and in all areas where feeling connected is important? Can you sustain an intimate relationship, confronting and resolving points of stress, anxiety, or discord in the relationship and in the world around you? If you are able to experience the way problem areas affect your relationship and work them through with your partner, you are fortunate. The abuse you experienced as a child had no meaningful impact on you, and maybe you should pass this book along to someone who may be less fortunate.

I have known a few people who, for reasons I frankly don't understand, have not experienced emotional disruption even though they were abused. There may be many others who were not hurt, but those who are comfortable in their intimate relationships are not the ones who come into treatment.

I am amazed that many people I see are functional at all, given the degree of trauma they have experienced. Yet there are men and women who are fully functional and come into counseling to work on particular concerns of a relatively ordinary nature. They are not denying that they were sexually abused, or repressing, displacing, or even lying about the fact. Somehow, in each of these individuals, the inner core of the individual has survived pretty much intact.

Actually, that is probably true for most of you. It is the level of a person's pain that argues against the notion of intactness: A history of blocking the pain is far more serious and, frankly, longer term work in therapy because a client must gain access to feelings before they can be worked through. Defenses become like fortresses and resist being broken down.

What is a "normal" environment? A normal — that is, healthy — environment is a family situation in which there is at least one parent or interested adult whom children can freely approach with questions, concerns, or sexual experiences in the full knowledge that the adult will address the questions, concerns, or experience with the children's welfare in mind. This does not mean that children are obligated to share, but that sharing is an option. In this situation, no trusted older individual violates the child's person, and the child feels the freedom to say no to a potential abuser and report the incident with full confidence that he or she will be believed and protected.

Without those circumstances there has to be a degree of stress in the parent-child relationship that is greater than the usual developmental push-pull of, "I want to do it *my* way."

Although sexual abuse may be described as having overt and covert forms, it is important to recognize that the impact of abuse is not necessarily categorized quite so neatly. It is also true that in situations where there is overt abuse, there are usually covert factors as well. In circumstances where there is no actual physical contact, the fear of it or the fantasy of it may have the same impact as if the experience had occurred.

As in all other experiences, the way you *feel* about what happened to you is as critical as the experience itself. That is why different individuals in the same family react so differently to the same situation.

This book will show how the results of childhood sexual abuse can be addressed and how steps can be taken to move past the impact. Short-term effects can be treated at the time of the experience. Long-term effects can only be partially treated at the initial disclosure. And there are some effects that are only realized when something happens to trigger them. This book will address all these aspects with particular attention to the way childhood experiences play themselves out — and can be treated — in adulthood.

1

What Is Sexual Abuse?

Sexual abuse is any experience or attitude imposed on an individual that gets in the way of the development of healthy sexual responses or behaviors. When you feel comfortable with your body, with your sexual preference, and with the physical expression of affection with another person, you are manifesting healthy responses or behaviors. These responses or behaviors also relate to the ease with which you establish close nonsexual relationships with both men and women.

An experience or attitude can be called abusive without its being either continuous or profound. For many people, a single traumatic event that gets blocked out of consciousness will have serious repercussions later on. I know of no one who

1

has experienced several or continual sexually abusive episodes who has walked away unscathed.

A great deal has been written about human sexuality and its implications. It is clearly one of the most complicated aspects of the human condition. Sexual attitudes are determined by many factors, including culture, society, peer group, and family. Sexual attitudes of the 1950s were vastly different from those of the 1960s. Certainly the public health hazards of the 1980s have had a drastic impact on sexual behaviors and attitudes.

Variants of culture and societal values may or may not cause emotional discomfort in some individuals. If those values get in the way of one's healthy psychosexual development, they can cause problems requiring adaptation or treatment. If they do not, the practices may be unacceptable to the larger culture, but they probably need not be judged as abusive.

What Is *Not* Sexual Abuse?

With the recent public awareness and exposure of sexual abuse to children, some overreaction and overconcern exist. It is very important to put all of these in proper perspective. It is as essential to recognize what is *not* sexual abuse as to know what is.

1. Prepuberty exploration among siblings is not to be encouraged but is not incest.
2. Children need to be hugged and held. Inappropriate hugging and holding is not hard to determine; it involves parts of the body we consider private.
3. At certain stages parents and children become aware of each other in sexual terms. These feelings get repressed, and both get past them. This often occurs at the onset of puberty when the child is still relatively unconscious sexually.
4. Bathing children until they are able to bathe themselves is not sexually abusive. Neither is washing the genital area when changing a diaper.

Concerned parents worry about the fine line between comfortable levels of undress and inappropriate exposure. They worry about the difference between complimenting a child on his or her appearance and being seductive. If you grew up in a household where the boundaries were unclear and the relationships were unclear, you may have difficulties knowing what is appropriate.

Normal Psychosexual Development

Without an understanding of what normal psychosexual development is all about, it is easy to develop shame around natural impulses.

Babies explore their bodies and find it pleasurable. The injunctions, "You will go blind if you masturbate," or "It will grow hair on your hands," make children unsettled. Explaining to children that some things are to be done in privacy gives a healthier message.

When children reach puberty and see their parents as sexual, and if they don't know that wanting your parent for your lover is a natural part of growing up, they can develop shame to the degree that they identify with those who have experienced incest. "I have no memory of sexual abuse, but I identify with the feelings of shame."

When parents become aware of the change in the body of a child and the child is sexually naive and still runs around scantily dressed or still wants to sit on Daddy's lap, the father may panic at his impulses and push the child away. The child feels rejected. "My daddy loved me until I became a woman and then he pulled away from me. What's wrong with me?"

Nothing is wrong, of course. But without an understanding of psychosexual development, the father sees himself as a "dirty old man," and the child feels that she has become unlovable. In fact, the child needs to be told that she has an adult body and that the rules have to change.

Inappropriate Behaviors

It is clearly inappropriate to be involved with your children in a way that is sexually arousing to you. Other behaviors may be less clear. Ask about them. Ask your child's pediatrician or someone you are fairly certain is concerned with these matters in a professional way. Don't judge yourself for not knowing, but don't avoid asking because you believe it is something you should know. Parents need to be educated in this phase of parenting, as well as in other aspects. Being a good parent is a very difficult task at best, and not having role models makes it even harder. It is worth noting that I *never* have seen a client suffering from the impact of sexual abuse in his or her life where the precipitating attitudes or behaviors were not clearly inappropriate. There has been no room for alternate interpretation. It is very unusual for a client to fabricate a story of sexual abuse without there being another reason that has nothing to do with that experience. My clinical experience has been clearly the reverse. Clients of mine have minimized experiences that have many implications that outrage me. Not only have they minimized them, but for many the abuse they suffered was so pervasive that they were unable to distinguish which of those behaviors were damaging to their sexual well-being.

Sigmund Freud is, of course, the most significant example of the "great minimizer." Recent disclosures indicate that since he could not accept the idea that so many of his patients had experienced incest, he determined that the incidents they reported were part of their fantasy life. This myth has been perpetuated until recently and probably retarded awareness in this critical area. The reality is that the numbers of individuals — both men and women — who have been sexually violated in one form or another by both men and women is staggering, regardless of whether or not we want to believe it.

There is an unbalance in writings on psychology about who gets molested and by whom. Although some allowances are made for variation, the literature primarily discusses boundary violations between fathers and daughters. It is clear to me that a thorough discussion of child sexual abuse cannot be limited to that one situation. Sexual abuse of children includes boys and girls, and the abusers are men and women and older children. The experience is very widespread.

This book will not attempt to define the number because statistics don't change anything. This book will treat the pain that results from these experiences for both men and women.

Overt or Covert Sexually Abusive Behaviors

Sexually abusive behaviors can be either overt or covert. There are overt behaviors that involve physical contact; there are covert behaviors that are sexually explicit; and there are those that have an impact on emotional life but are more subtle. These relate more to what has been labeled emotional abuse or enmeshment. In some instances, it is hard to separate them from one another. It is also hard to determine exactly what happens as a result of what. Covert and overt abuse can exist at the same time. Overt abuse invariably involves some covert activity as well. Covert abuse of an emotional nature can be a lot more subtle and more difficult to pinpoint. It does not necessarily involve anything that is sexually explicit. People who have experienced covert abuse will identify emotionally with others who have been sexually abused but will often be confused as to why they do. There is probably no single event but rather an attitude that is disruptive in nature.

2

Sexually Abusive Behaviors

It is important for you to have an idea of what constitutes sexually abusive behaviors. Ironically enough, if you grew up with sexual abuse, it is entirely possible that you do not know what it is. That does not mean that you are either stupid or unaware. There is so much confusion around appropriateness in a dysfunctional household that sexually abusive behaviors may not be considered relevant. How often have I heard from a client, "I just had something flash through my head. I don't know if it means anything but . . ." That fragment is invariably a key to a critical insight.

Many of these sexually abusive behaviors are blatant and overt. Many are much more subtle. All are damaging to the child. All carry with them consequences that need to be addressed. Because I discuss them separately does not mean that the behaviors are necessarily separate.

I remember working with a young man in his early thirties who was still a virgin. He was unhappy about this but terrified to move beyond the stage of petting with clothes on. He had no concerns about his parts working or his ability to work his parts but something clearly got in his way. One day, just as he broke into a sweat over this issue, he had a memory flash. "I don't know if this means anything," he said, "but when I was about eleven or twelve, the boys at school started tossing around words I hadn't heard before. I was curious about what they meant, but I couldn't ask because I had to pretend that I knew. When I got home, I asked my father. He was drunk, and I guess I should have known better, but I was very curious.

"My father said, 'I'll do better than tell you. I'll show you.' He proceeded to take out a pornographic magazine and pointed out places between a woman's legs that I had never seen before. I looked in amazement, frozen to the spot.

"The next thing I remember was being in my room, sick to my stomach. It only happened that once. Do you think that it's connected?"

This young man had no idea that what his father had done was sexually abusive and had set up an aversive attitude toward the naked female body. The realization that he had been abused was his beginning step in overcoming the problem.

The largest number of reported cases of child sexual abuse are parent or other family members to child. I use the terms "sexually abusive behavior" and "incest" interchangeably in an attempt to give "incest" a broader meaning. As I define it, incest refers to anyone in the child's life who is in a position of authority and can exert power, including a teacher, a parent's boyfriend or girlfriend, or family members.

Overt Sexual Behaviors

Overt sexual behaviors include inappropriate nudity; for example, an adult walking around the house without any clothes on or an adult standing in the doorway of a child's room unannounced in an attempt to catch the child in the process of getting undressed or being undressed is abusive. It is an invasion of boundaries. Kissing the child on the lips in a lingering way reserved for adult relationships and fondling the child's genital areas are abusive. Masturbating in front of the child, using the child to assist in masturbation, or masturbating the child is abusive. Oral involvement with a child of either sex is abusive whether it is done to the child or the child is forced to engage in it with the adult. Putting a finger or a penis or other object into the child's anus or vagina is abusive. Dry intercourse is another example of abusive behavior.

Subtle Sexual Abuse

The following are examples of more subtle sexual abuse. Although there may be no physical contact, there is a crossing of the boundaries that allows persons to develop independently and experience their own sexuality. The adult interferes with the child's sexual development and directs it toward the adult rather than toward individuation. The dynamic is powerful.

- A man reported that whenever he planned to go out on a date, his mother always got sick, and he would feel tremendously guilty if he left her.
- "My mother and I slept in the same room until I left home in my middle thirties."
- "My father used to trail me when I went out on a date."
- "My father used to insult my friends so that they wouldn't come back."
- "When my mother drank, she would become seductive with me although she didn't touch me. I would become aroused, and that panicked me so that I actually became impotent when I was seventeen."
- "I was called pet names of Slut, Bitch, Whore and most often She Dog. This was my whole life until I finally left home at twenty."
- "I was accused of trying to seduce my father when I was five and after."

- "My mother was always jealous of my girlfriends."
- "I would always be accused of immoral acts when I came home from a date."
- "It disturbed me that my father held me in higher esteem than he did my mother. I was more his wife than she was. I was also a better housekeeper."
- "I was afraid I would be physically or sexually abused although I never was."
- "I was given graphic descriptions of my parents' sex life."
- "I was told in very crude ways how women seduce men and men seduce women."
- "I was told that they really wanted a boy, and I was always treated like a boy. I stole my first bras and had many dreams about erasing my breasts."
- "My mother told me she thought about me all the time. I feel guilty because I didn't think about her all the time."
- "My mom and I are very close. When I heard the sounds of my father abusing my mom it felt like it was me."
- "When my father came home drunk, he would strip, beat, and rape my mother. I would pretend to be asleep. I was terrified that if he became aware of me, I would be next. I was so powerless."

What has been listed here is by no means complete. It is a sampling of the nature of what we hear regularly from those who have a history of sexual abuse.

3

Dysfunctional Family Systems

Although those who sexually abuse others are clearly emotionally disturbed, it also should be acknowledged that rarely does this manifest itself without the proper conditions. By this, I mean that the family is already dysfunctional in some regard. For example, the system in which alcoholism is present is a perfect setting for this to occur. The alcoholism or other dysfunction itself does not cause an individual to become sexually abusive; what happens is that the situation makes it easier for these symptoms to play themselves out.

Five Factors Accompanying Alcoholism

1. Blurring of Boundaries

It is not unusual for a child to be confused as to what is okay to feel and what is not okay to feel. Confusion creates a climate that allows boundary blurring to occur; it does not occur in a more orderly environment.

2. Denial

There is so much lying that goes on in so many different forms that it becomes difficult for a child to recognize the truth. The denial that what is going on is really going on is pervasive. Children who report seeing a drunken parent, for example, are quite often told that what they say they saw they did not see. It is much easier to deny than to face what is real. Denial helps create a climate in which the child is confused as to what is really happening and what is really going on.

3. Inconsistent Nurture

In an environment where children inconsistently have their needs met, there is an ever present hunger. Children crave attention. They crave nurture. They do not really care about the nature of the attention or the nurture they receive. They will do anything they can in order to receive it.

4. Poor Self-Image

Children in alcoholic family systems grow up believing that they are responsible for anything and everything that goes wrong. They're not good enough. Others may make mistakes but they *are* a mistake. Therefore, they deserve anything that happens to them. Anything that happens to them to some degree was caused because their very existence has caused difficulty for others. Thus, any sexual abuse is also their fault because they caused it. If they were not shameful and were not bad, the abuse would not have happened. It is further evidence that there is something inherently wrong with them.

5. Lack of Information
About How Healthy Families Function

The consequence is lack of information about how to function in a healthy family. Lack of information can be a set-up for abuse. A therapist told me the following story. She was working with a family of four including mother, father, and two children, ages six and four. In a conversation with the children, the therapist learned that every night the youngest girl would come into her parents' bedroom and lie down on the bed between them. Shortly thereafter, the older girl would enter the bedroom and lie down on the floor beside the bed. At this point the mother would get out of the bed and go out of the room with the older child, leaving the younger child in bed with the father. Nothing inappropriate had happened, but, in the opinion of the therapist, if the father could not maintain his sobriety the child was at risk.

The therapist also knew from the mother that she did not want to be touched by her husband and took the arrival of the children as a way to get out of the bedroom. As a result, she was encouraging this behavior to become habitual. Children enjoy coming into bed with parents. It is to be discouraged except in a limited way from time to time. In this circumstance, the children were getting their needs met, the mother was finding a way to take care of herself, and the child was at risk.

First, we are looking at the fact that this is a system where alcoholism is present. When alcohol is present, we have to look at three generations, and the next step was to look for more alcoholism. A look at the family history showed that the parents also came from homes where there was alcoholism. The parents were both Adult Children of Alcoholics. The therapist knew that as a result they were very limited in their understanding or awareness of appropriate boundaries and appropriate parenting.

This is important information. It means that an intervention could be educational. The couple was counseled with an eye toward developing boundaries within the family. The goal of the couple's therapy was to talk about appropriate parenting and child-parent behaviors. It opened up an arena for discussing the idea that the children do not belong in their parents' bed and that this is not a good idea for anybody, regardless of whether or not there are future risks to the child's sexuality. The parents also needed to learn how to confront their problems directly. Children should not be put in the middle to ease marital discord.

The behavior stopped. The family is still distressed, but the problems have not been seriously compounded.

4

The Perpetrator

Any discussion of sexual abuse must pay some attention to the question, "What kind of person would do that to a child?"

Molestation: A Manifestation of Emotional Disturbance

We know that child molestation is a manifestation of emotional disturbance. The loss of impulse control that permits inappropriate sexual conduct is pathological in nature. This does *not* imply that an understanding of the sickness in any way makes people less accountable for their behavior. It does mean that rage at the perpetrator may be a necessary phase of recovery. As survivors of abuse go through the process of achieving wellness, they will have progressively more difficulty and less interest in trying to understand the profoundly distorted thinking of the perpetrator.

Awareness of Dynamics

Your awareness of some of these dynamics is important not because you need to understand the perpetrator. You probably have spent lots of time and energy trying to understand why, why me and why not someone else — going around and around in circles. Understanding what goes on in the minds of perpetrators is important only in regard to how their thinking and attitudes impact on you and how you internalize them.

It is not unusual to find that someone who sexually abuses a child was also sexually abused as a child. To a healthy mind, that makes no sense at all. Nevertheless, it is true in the same way that those who physically abuse their children and spouses were invariably physically abused themselves. But the fact that you were sexually abused does *not* mean you will become an abuser. The explanation for this lies not in the specific behavior but in the psychological attitude.

The perpetrators I have spoken to were rarely — prior to treatment — conscience-stricken about the event or events. They came into treatment primarily because the leverage applied was too great to resist; for example, they were threatened with jail or loss of family. Often a perpetrator is incredulous and wonders why everybody is making such a big deal out of this. "After all, I didn't hurt him (her). It stopped as soon as it came out. Why can't we work this out as a family the way we did the alcoholism? It has nothing to do with my relationship with my wife."

The sorrow the perpetrator expresses is in getting caught and facing consequences — not in having damaged another human being. The desire to "work this out" is a desire to get off the hook, not to understand the impact of the behavior. The perpetrator's attitude takes no one else's feelings into account. The victim is merely an object placed there by the perpetrator to be used for his own purpose.

Even if the perpetrator expresses remorse after the lid is blown off, it is still only in terms of the self. "I did a bad thing and I'm sorry. I won't do it again. Can you forgive me?" I *never* hear a perpetrator ask, directly or indirectly, "What were you feeling? What do you feel like inside? How can I help ease *your* pain?"

This focus is critical and cannot be minimized. It puts the spotlight back on the perpetrator and leaves the feelings of the victim unaddressed. Victims are unaware of this focus and will respond to the fact that the perpetrator is sorry . . . won't do it again . . . never intended to hurt, etc., without realizing that they are once again not tending to their own needs but are taking care of the perpetrator.

Since the emotional level is so high and the remorse is so real, victims are fooled into believing the connection is serving them. In reality, it is only the intensity of the moment, and once the moment is passed, the empty feeling will surface once again.

It is best if victims can go *immediately* into therapy, if only not to lose the focus on what they experienced in terms of self. The stress is on *immediate* because if much time is allowed to lapse, there is a real good chance you will once again shut down or numb out, making treatment more difficult. The intensity of the moment will permit access to feelings. Addressing those feelings will help them to begin to heal.

It is important that you understand these perpetrator reactions because these are the messages you receive and internalize. One of the reasons why the "secret" does not get out is because you minimize as well. "It only happened once . . . I wasn't hurt . . . He told me I was beautiful . . . She said she loved me." All of this plays into the needy psyche of the child and makes it easier not to face the consequences and repercussions of blowing the whistle.

The denial system remains intact if there is no intervention to crack it open.

5

The Enablers

Some parents are truly unaware of what is going on. The secret is so carefully kept that there is no indication that something is wrong, and therefore, the possibility does not enter the mind of the other parent. Even if there are signs of depression in the child, the causes are attributed elsewhere.

An emotionally unavailable parent will greet the information with denial and minimize it in an attempt to make it go away and not upset the balance in the family.

A caring parent discovering the abuse will be overwhelmed with guilt and rage. Emotionally devastated, the parent will move in to nurture and protect the child. Whether the parent who discovers the abuse is emotionally unavailable or caring, the family system will be seriously disrupted.

The impact of sexual abuse is far-reaching. Other family members are certain to be affected. Even though other family members may not be the principal players in the event, their concerns, fears, guilt, and anger are also important. It is not possible for life to go on as if nothing has happened. There has to be an impact, regardless of whether it is addressed or not addressed.

For many people the post-trauma experience is just as devastating as the incest itself. Regardless of how badly they are treated, children cannot dismiss their parents as merely powerful figures whose approval they seek. Their need for the love of a parent persists even if they were abused by that parent. When molestation stops, the child gets cut off from interaction with that parent. Movement toward the child by that parent will cause the child to panic. The parent's movement away from the child is experienced by the child as abandonment, so that the child is left with a sick, empty feeling inside. Abuse has an impact on the rest of the family members in terms of both their response to the victim and the perpetrator and their feelings about being a part of a family where this occurs.

A few weeks ago Lillian was sobbing hysterically about the fact that her sister was sexually abused by their father and that she hadn't even known about it earlier. She felt so much pain for her sister and so much pain for herself. She was racked with guilt — maybe there were clues that she had missed; oh, if she had only known. Lillian was speaking of a time when she was nine (clearly the parent in the family) and her sister was seven.

"What could you have done if you had known?"

"I would have put an end to it. I would have been there for her. I would have . . . I thought we were close, and yet she didn't tell me."

It is hard to know what she would have or could have done had she known. It is important to recognize that she was projecting backward onto the nine-year-old the strengths she had gained after two years of therapy. It is important for her to return to that age and her feelings at that age in order to recall what was going on in her internal world and her sister's to cause her sister to keep the secret. Once she had retured to that time, it became important to develop the story line in order to gain a sense of (1) what would have happened had she told, (2) what the results of that would have been, and (3) how that would have been handled.

She fantasized that she could have protected her little sister and shielded her from the pain. Two little girls huddled together in a corner, clinging to each other.

Now that Lillian and her sister are working on their present connection, they will have an opportunity to share all those feelings and to put the responsibility where it belongs — outside of them.

6

Coping Responses

Since the experience of sexual abuse is so bizarre, coping mechanisms may also appear bizarre. It is of value to recognize that adaptive behaviors to maladaptive experiences may, under other circumstances, be considered signs of emotional instability. In the instance of sexual abuse, adaptive behaviors serve a very definite purpose: they help you to survive. It is critical that this be understood. If the behaviors persist when the environment changes, the survival skills will no longer serve a good purpose and will require treatment.

Resistance

When the abuse begins, many victims will try to fight off the perpetrator. The resistance can lead to further abuse.

"I fought and it only made matters worse. If I had fought harder, I would have gotten killed; so I stopped fighting.

"Now when someone is aggressive with me, I get stuck. I am powerless to stick up for myself. I can't even figure out what I should do."

Lack of Resistance

Sometimes children are led to believe that the abuse is a gesture of love and will not resist. For many, it is the only form of affection that they get; thus, they will hunger for it and willingly participate. It will make them feel special. Trusting an adult is in the nature of being a child. Many children do, however, resist. Runaways, by and large, are children who have been abused and saw no other way out. Many others who are unable to escape the situation physically take to emotional flight. Quite often this response is seen as compliance. It is not. It is compliance of body but not of spirit. Since the child sees no way to escape, the mind adapts.

Emotional Shutdown

For some children, the psychic pain is so intolerable that the child shuts down all emotions and literally feels nothing. This shutting down to all stressful situations becomes an automatic response that carries into adulthood. One of the results is to deny that the impact of the abuse was profound. Survivors will, therefore, discuss stressful situations as if they were observers and not participants. Survivors also lack awareness of what a stressful situation is, which leads to minimizing the severity of the early experience and of other experiences that would ordinarily evoke strong feelings.

It is crucial for you to begin to learn, at least on a cognitive level, what experiences warrant what responses. I tell my clients when they report horror stories without emotion what my reaction would have been or is. For example, "If that happened to me I'd be outraged." Or, "Oh, how terribly sad."

At first, survivors are amazed at my response and then will check for the same effect somewhere inside themselves.

Don't be surprised if you can't get to it. Since these feelings are so deeply buried, it is not unusual for the first feeling that surfaces to be one of anxiety. "What will happen if all the other feelings surface?"

"If I start to cry, will I ever be able to stop?"

"If I start to feel the rage, will I lose control?"

These fears are understandable, but bear in mind that if shutting down is your way of coping, you can probably do it at will. It will be relatively easy to put back the lid. Letting the feelings out is the hard part. *Remember this: the feelings do not have to come out all at once — little by little is just fine.*

Dissociative Behavior

Some people find that although they are unable to remove their body from the trauma, they can leave emotionally. Therefore, they split mind and soul from body and go somewhere else. They give up the physical self and enter a fantasy life. In adulthood this coping mechanism will result in *dissociative behavior* — "spacing out" — in stressful situations.

"Where did you go?"

"Sorry, I didn't hear you."

One woman reported staring at a painting on the wall when she was continuously abused by her father and two brothers. Now, as an adult, when she is under stress, she begins to hallucinate that picture and the objects in the picture will move and talk. Many people report these kinds of experiences.

Amnesia

Another form of dissociative behavior is *amnesia*. The abuse is just too awful to remember, and because it is just not possible to separate it all out, all memory is lost. Some people who have been abused will develop multiple personalities. One personality will know what went on and another personality will have no recollection of it, whatsoever.

Preserving Bodily Integrity

The body goes to great lengths to preserve its integrity. These extreme responses are ways to manage an otherwise unmanageable situation. Persons dissociate themselves from the situation because there is no way to acknowledge what is really happening.

Professional help provides the best route to *integration.* It is very hard for people with this response to integrate by themselves.

Blocking Out the Experience

One way to cope is to block out the experience as if it never happened. The mind, in order to protect itself from the power of the psychic trauma, *represses* the memory of the event(s). It is not unusual for people to have no memory of several years in their childhood.

Identifying With Others

It is not uncommon for someone to *identify* with other survivors of sexual abuse but not know why. "I know something happened, but I can't recall what it is no matter how hard I try."

Returning Memories

When the memories begin to return, they will return in a couple of ways. Someone will share an experience, and there will be a familiar ring to it. Many times the unconscious responds first with a dream. Memory of the dream will initiate memories being brought to the conscious level.

If memory is not critical to resolution of a current crisis, it is fine to let this process of regaining memory take its own time. Remembering the dreams is usually a sign of readiness to process the material. Keep a pad and pencil by your bed so that you can write them down as soon as you awaken. Memories of dreams fade very quickly.

Trust your hunches. If you think there is a connection, there probably is. If you are open to the discovery, chances are it will reveal itself. The content may be different from what you suppose, but it will surface.

I remember a woman who was certain she had been sexually abused by her alcoholic father but was just as certain that he had never laid a hand on her. It caused her concern because of her identification with others whose personal boundaries had been violated. One night she had a flashback. "I don't know if this means anything," she said, "but here goes. When my father was drunk, he would station himself in the bathroom and sit on the side of the tub. He was immovable. Since we only had one bathroom and you could hold it for only so long, you would be forced to use the toilet and listen to his abusive comments as he glared at you. It was awful. And there was no moving him."

She had no idea until the memory surfaced and she was able to share it that this behavior was abusive to her sexuality. The experience induced shame about her body and its normal functions.

Awareness: The Key to Resolution

The awareness of what is sexually abusive is critical to resolving the impact of it. The memory without the links and the understanding of its implications limit its value. I know that when I am discussing these issues with a client, that person will not be able to hear me if what I am saying is very close to a core issue. The spacing-out response is swift and automatic. In the controlled environment of a clinical session, it can be addressed and dealt with. The closer the comment is to the core issue, the harder it is to see or hear it. For example, a client when asked, "What did I just say?" may respond, "Huh? I'm sorry, would you say it again? It must be important because I lost the whole thing."

What this reaction suggests is that under stress these coping mechanisms immediately come into play and set the individual up to be victimized again because there is no conscious awareness of the danger. The psychic protection takes over, and the person is put at risk.

In other words, these individuals are, for example, easily set up for date rape or other physical abuse. It means that if there are clues to the potential danger, they are not heeded.

This is *not* to suggest that the individual bears any responsibility for the assault. However, it offers a way to look at two questions often asked: "What is there about me that makes these terrible things happen over and over?" and "Am I self-destructive?"

The answer to both questions is quite simple. "Your warning light does not go on, so you don't see the risks that would be known to others."

Common Aspects of Coping Mechanisms

One aspect that all coping mechanisms have in common is that the person is at risk to continue in the victim role. The person doesn't see the danger for what it is and either doesn't respond at all or fantasizes about what is happening in order to feel safe.

On the first morning of a workshop, some of the members shared feelings with the group and others did not. This is entirely predictable behavior. People pace themselves differently.

The following morning one woman told the group that she had made herself vulnerable the day before and would have been angry at the group members who had not shared, had she not realized that they would have shared had there been more time. Her anger was fleeting, and once she had made herself feel safe, she shut down any discomfort around the experience.

"Wait a minute," I said. "You have just set yourself up to be hurt. In order for you to feel safe, you fantasized the feelings of some of the group members. If at another point you learn otherwise, you will feel like the victim. You will feel as if you've been had and you will have set yourself up. It is important to check out your assumptions."

In the checking out, she heard from the others.

"Yes, I would have shared, but we ran out of time."

"I made a special point of keeping quiet because I always jump in too fast."

"I didn't feel like talking. I just wanted to listen."

Up until this point she had played all of the parts. She had her reaction and decided what everyone else's was also. Knowing the truth made her feel safe. She could begin to accept the others for feeling as they did and could see that the consequence of being vulnerable is not always disaster. She did not have to fantasize in order to avoid feeling violated. If she gave up the fantasy, she could be more in control of her life experience. As she became conscious of ways in which fantasizing plays out, she had a better opportunity to change this response. This was a very simple example of a powerful dynamic that had been an ongoing problem for her.

A man I knew was very disturbed because his boss had not recommended him for a promotion that he knew he deserved. It was very clear when she hired him that his new boss also wanted him for a lover and had an agenda that included more than just how good a professional he would be.

She was not subtle, so he was aware of her feelings, but he decided that it did not have to be a problem. He decided that although he did not want to be her lover, they could be friends. He ran errands for her, took her sailing, gave her lifts when her car broke down, took her to dinner, but refused to share his body.

He felt victimized when she did not recommend him for a promotion because he believed that he did everything he could to please her. However, it wasn't enough. He had fulfilled all the professional criteria appropriate to gaining this promotion. Beyond that he had been her friend. What she wanted, he believed, was inappropriate, but she punished him anyway because he would not give in. Here again, he played both parts and decided for her how she would react. She obviously had a different script.

This man's childhood role was to take care of his mother. He felt like her father or her husband but never her son. As a young man he was so fearful of his mother's emotional and sexual demands that he became impotent. His body had found a way to manage the threat. Since the threat was too awful to contemplate, he split off from it on a conscious level and his body took over.

In the situation he faced as an adult, he split off from her reaction to his refusal and behaved in a very naive manner. He was not prepared to experience her wrath at his noncompliance just as he was never ready for his mother's hostility because he did not come through for her either.

Here again, he felt like the victim and was cast in the victim role because he was unable to utilize the warning signs. After all, in both situations he was a "good boy." If he could understand the warnings, chances are he would not have taken the job. Since he wanted the job, he denied the reality and decided that he could manage the problem. His fantasies masked the danger and made him feel safe.

Most of the time unchecked assumptions or daydreaming have no meaningful consequences. Since they have no meaningful consequences, your awareness of them needs to be heightened.

Protecting the Next Generation

One of the reasons why it is crucial for us to address some of these coping mechanisms is to protect the next generation. If symptoms go untreated, there is always the risk that they will play themselves out over and over again.

When Sheila called me on the phone, she was hysterical. She had just learned that her father had tried to sexually molest her daughter. "I can't believe it," she screamed. "He molested me, but I never thought he would also molest his grandchildren. What a monster he is!" she said. "I can't stand it! I wish he were dead. I wish I were dead. My poor daughter. How could I have let this happen?"

"Wait a minute," I said. "Let's take a look at what's going on and what can be done. Although you are incredulous at what happened, on some level you knew it could happen because you have done your best not to let your children be alone with him.

"Your daughter has something that you didn't have. Your daughter has you for a mother. She has the opportunity in this situation to come running to you knowing that she will be protected. She can come running knowing that something will happen to help her. You didn't have that.

"You are no longer shut down, and she does not have to shut down."

Sheila took immediate action. She went with her daughter to a therapist and in front of the therapist talked about how crazy her father was and about the way he had behaved all of her life. She made it very clear that her daughter had in no way instigated what had nearly happened. She then stated that her father would have to be confronted, and that it was long overdue. Next Sheila confronted her father with his behavior this time and all of the other times. She did it without fear of loss. Her mother left the room in disbelief, but Sheila no longer cared. The father's response was to admit what he had done. He had no guilt feelings about any of his behavior, but a part of him was somewhat relieved that it was over. He said, "I have been waiting for this." He had been waiting for thirty years.

The nightmare was over.

The untreated mother remains in denial. She was unable (1) to confront her husband, (2) to accept the reality of what had happened to her daughter or her granddaughter, and (3) to address it either for herself or for them.

I witnessed a far more subtle but no less damaging display of assault on the sexuality of an adolescent not too long ago. I stopped by with my friend Ronald and his daughter at a family gathering after the death of a mutual friend. I had always been curious as to why Ronald — whom I saw as capable, talented and desirable — saw himself as very ordinary and certainly not worthy of a relationship with anyone who was his peer. It had never made sense to me. On this day the reason became clear.

We entered the home where the gathering was taking place. Ronald introduced me to his uncle, who then looked at his daughter and called her by her sister's name. Ronald's uncle had known the girl for nineteen years. Another relative introduced herself and then made a comment to the girl about "the strange way all you kids are wearing your hair these days." I was beginning to tense up. At that moment, another relative came by, patted Ronald's daughter on her behind, gave her a little wink and walked away. That did it. Ronald's daughter had been standing there the whole time, nonresponsive. It was as if she were frozen to the spot.

My friend seemed totally oblivious to any of this going on. I was not. I said to Ronald, "I am getting out of here — either with you or without you — and your daughter is coming with me."

I took my coat, said goodbye to those I had to say goodbye to and headed for the door. He came after us. Outside he said to me, "What's wrong with you? What happened? What's making you so crazy?"

"Can you be that oblivious? Didn't you hear and see what just happened to your daughter? Can you really let people treat her that way?"

Ronald turned to me. "What are you talking about?"

"Your uncle doesn't remember her name. Your sister criticizes the way she wears her hair. Another relative feels free to pat her on the backside and give her a suggestive wink, and that's okay with you?"

Ronald stood there, humiliated. Tears came to his eyes. He reached out to his daughter, put his arms around her, and said, "Oh my God. I have lived with them my whole life, and what I have learned to do in order to protect myself is simply to turn them off. I don't hear a word they say. I don't know how many years ago I stopped, but I no longer listen. There was never anything they said that made me feel good, so I literally shut them out. I guess what I did was shut out all of their remarks, and — God forgive me — I shut out what they were saying to you as well."

He turned to me and thanked me for making him aware. Then he turned to his daughter and gave her his solemn promise that that kind of abuse would never, ever happen to her again if he had any say about it.

She started to minimize. He put his finger to her lips and stopped her. They cried in each other's arms. Once again a coping mechanism that had been essential for survival at one time had later become the enemy.

Coping Mechanisms Can Be Changed

These responses or coping mechanisms can be changed. You can work on them initially by doing mental exercises to force yourself to stay focused. Chances are you daydream on the job or in the classroom. Do exercises that are designed to improve your powers of concentration.

Chances are you make assumptions about others' attitudes and feelings toward you without checking them out. You can't really know how someone else feels unless you ask.

People have many different ways of coping when their stress buttons are pushed. I have one group that includes one person who will go glassy-eyed, one who will fall asleep, at least two who will start stuffing their faces, and another who will flee to the bathroom. When the subject affects the entire group, the scene is something to behold. Since their awareness has been heightened, they know what they are doing and can bring themselves back. They also can be amused by their behaviors and not beat themselves "for not being done with this already."

A supportive and nurturing group and possibly some individual work will help to speed up the integration process. It is important for mind, feelings, and body to be congruent. That is part of everyone's lifelong process of becoming mature.

7

Impact

The impact of childhood sexual abuse is best described as having three different effects. First are the short-term or immediate effects. Second are the long-term effects. Third is the time bomb or the situational effects.

Short-Term, Immediate Effects

Sense of Being Damaged and Low Self-Esteem

Questions such as these two persist:

1. Will I be normal?
2. If I marry, will my husband know?

Some of these sexually abused children have experienced pain. Some have had venereal diseases. Some have had abortions or have carried babies to term. This type of abuse makes children believe they will never be clean or whole. They have a sense of being damaged and, therefore, not worth much. Because of these and other negative feelings to be discussed, children think very poorly of themselves, become isolated, and believe they are undesirable and unworthy.

Guilt and Shame

Children feel guilt and shame because of what happened. They feel guilty if there is disclosure. They feel guilty if there is disruption in the family as a result of disclosure. They feel shame because they "caused it."

Fear and Lack of Trust

Children live in constant fear of abuse and in fear of reprisals if there is any resistance to the abuse. There is no place to run and no one to run to. How can anyone be trusted if such a betrayal can occur?

Depression and Anger

Sexually abused children have many suicidal thoughts and may attempt suicide. The depression can become chronic. Repressed anger and hostility are disguised as passivity and compliance. Both of these are forms of depression in which anger is turned inward.

Confused Role Boundaries

The child is not the child. The child is "parentified," that is, cast in the role of parent. There is enmeshment between parent and child.

Uneven Child Development

There is an appearance of maturity, but the child does not develop as children need to. In fact, there has been no childhood.

Sense of Powerlessness

Children internalize the sense that they have no rights, have no privacy, and exist to be abused by a more powerful person.

Long-Term Effects

All of the Untreated Childhood Effects

These effects will persist into adulthood and become more generalized if left untreated. They include guilt and shame, anger and rage, and loss, as well as violations of both physical and psychological boundaries.

Postpuberty Responses to Early Sexual Experience

The early sexual experience gets reframed in light of more adult responses to sex.

Compulsive Behavior

This category includes alcohol and drug abuse, sexual addictions, eating disorders, self-mutilation, and relationship addictions.

Posttraumatic Stress Disorder

A few months or years after the abuse, the coping mechanisms will cease to function and symptoms will surface.

Lack of Models

There is no frame of reference for the development of healthy intimate relationships.

Developmental Triggers

Normal occurrences can call into play an area of functioning that has been impaired because of the abuse and reveal developmental gaps that pseudomaturity has successfully hidden.

Time-Bomb or Situational Effects

Misdiagnosis

There is a time-bomb effect with many responses so that there is no way to predict how the trauma will manifest itself in the adult world.

8

Guilt

Guilt feelings seem to be universally accepted as something to be overcome. And yet interestingly enough, *guilt* is part of the human condition. It is the way civilization passes on its mores. It is a way that parents use to get children to conform, and these children then carry this response into adulthood. In turn, they induce guilt in their own children, and the pattern continues. As we mature, *conscience* takes the place of guilt. Guilt exists outside of the self; conscience exists within the self.

Guilt involves the need for approval from another or others and makes one think twice about certain behaviors, usually after the fact. Conscience becomes a deterrent. This deterrent occurs when one's values are known at least to oneself.

It is not desirable to eliminate guilt or conscience about behaviors altogether; anyone without some of these feelings is a sociopath. Your conscience is an integral part of your personality. With the aid of conscience, you establish and develop a value system and, subsequently, an outline for life.

In healthy families, the norms are clear and consistent. The consequences are predictable and exist primarily for the benefit of the child and the perpetuation of the system.

In unhealthy families the norms are less clear. The appropriate and acceptable behaviors are not consistently modeled. The consequences, too, are inconsistent. When they exist, they are not for the benefit of the child but largely for displacement of anger or reduction of embarrassment caused by the child being reported by the school, the police, or a neighbor.

"How could you do this to me?" is the guilt inducer. Thus, the consequence for children is that their behavior is corrected for their growth and development. But there's more. The parents' inability to cope results in the children having to fix it for their parents. As a result, children are not only children but also parents to their parents. The only answer is not to be a child — not to act out.

Translation of Guilt

The guilt induced translates not only into feeling bad for creating problems for someone else but also in a peculiar sense of power. For example, I have the power to devastate and only then can I make it okay again. The devastation in reality is not caused by the child but is triggered by the child. This is a critical difference that is not understood by the child. The power is distorted because it exists only when the parent abdicates.

The guilt involved in causing problems for someone else is appropriate and healthy for the development of a responsible person. "I had to leave work early to go to your school to talk to your teachers about your not doing your homework. I got punished and I did nothing wrong." An awareness that irresponsible behavior does not exist in isolation and affects other people is part of the maturation process.

The idea is not to feel guilty about the things for which you are not responsible or over which you have no control. For example, as I write this I am about to fly home. If the plane is late, those meeting me will be inconvenienced. I can feel bad for their inconvenience and my own, but to feel guilty is inappropriate since I have no control over the landing time and am powerless to change it.

Adults who have been sexually abused as children carry guilt. Many have been in therapy for long periods of time and still hang onto the guilt. Intellectually, they know all the right answers, but that kind of knowledge doesn't change anything. They read all the books and articles about how the child, regardless of the child's behavior, has no responsibility. However, knowing doesn't change anything.

Guilt as a Way of Adapting

There must be a deeper reason to hang onto the guilt. The guilt itself must be of some benefit to the survival mechanism. Guilt is a part of the way that many adapt.

The child who is sexually abused is overwhelmed with feelings of helplessness, powerlessness, sadness, and anger. The child questions, "Why me? Why would someone want to do this to me? What will become of me?"

You must find an answer in order to survive emotionally. The child's answer is, "This is happening because of me. It is my fault and I am getting what I deserve." As awful as this is to contemplate, this affords the child a sense of control. It is preferable to feel responsible for the horror than to feel totally powerless in the presence of it.

Distortion

Distortion is essential for many to remain sane. Losing touch with what is real may be the only way to function in the real world.

A student of mine had been sexually molested by a teacher. The event had occurred when she had returned to

the classroom for something she had forgotten. She had
carried around guilt about this for twenty years. She said, "I
could have gotten along without the book. I could have run
in and out. I didn't have to stop. When he said, 'There's
something I want to show you in the coat closet,' I didn't
have to go. I could have . . ."

All the therapy focused on the idea that she was the child,
he was the adult, and it was *not* her fault hadn't helped.
There had to be something in it for her to hang onto the
guilt. It had to serve a purpose. If it were true that she was not
guilty, then she was powerless to prevent it. And the idea of
total powerlessness was absolutely intolerable to her. It was
better to feel guilty than to be overwhelmed by a sense of
helplessness. No wonder she hung onto the guilt. It was the
only power that she had.

The guilt had served a purpose. It probably had protected
her sanity. As an adult, she no longer finds the guilt in that
encounter useful. As an adult she does not ever again have to
be the victim. She can learn ways to have real power. She can
develop tools. She is not defenseless. She can walk away.
She can call out. She can confront. She can do whatever is
necessary.

Once she can feel confident that she is in charge of what
happens to her body, she can then let go of the guilt that she
carries because of the childhood experience. She can accept
the powerlessness of that child, rid herself of the onus of
responsibility, feel compassion and love for herself, and
move on from there.

Guilt may be power for the victim, but tools for living are
the power for the survivor.

9

Guilt and Shame

John said, "I've been at my job for less than a month, and a new job offer has come through that I really want. I've agreed to take it and I feel so guilty. What will I say to my boss? What will he think of me? How can I do that to him?"

Guilt

John can easily work on the guilt part of this situation. Feeling guilty is a habit. The automatic response to making anyone else feel uncomfortable is guilt. The truth is that John's response was more embarrassment at finding himself in this position than anything else. The guilt is a false sense of power.

"Remember the irony," I said to him. "Remember how they yanked your chain about your competition before they hired you, and now no one else can fill your shoes. Either they played games with you when they said that they had to choose between you and other qualified applicants or they told you you could be replaced." This was an ordinary reaction to a situation. The significant part of this interaction was when I asked John, "What will he think of you?"

John answered, "He will find me disgusting and beneath contempt." Those are not guilt words. Those are shame words. They are experienced at a deeper level.

Shame

John was a sexually abused child. He learned at a very early age that he was put on this earth to service and give pleasure to others. He was not allowed needs and desires of his own, and learned to repress all such feelings. When a want or desire surfaced, he would be so filled with self-loathing that he would dismiss it.

As a result of therapy, he began to realize that he had been abused and that he knew no other way to respond. Slowly he began to believe that it was okay to want for himself. Pleasing himself and acting in his own interests were not only acceptable but desirable.

This job was a dream job for John. It was precisely what he wanted to do, with a substantial raise and in a part of the country where he had always wanted to live. No wonder all the "old stuff" surfaced. His present boss took on a parent role in his emotional world, and he felt shameful that he was about to do something for himself. His boss is not the same person as his abusive parents. Yes, his boss will be disappointed, maybe even a little angry, but it is not as big a matter as he experiences it. The guilt part will be over after he confronts and addresses the issue. The shame part persists.

Early abuse, if left unresolved, will continue to be a deterrent to healthy growth patterns. Identification is a first step.

10

Shame

Shame has its roots in the essential identity of the person. The internalization is profound. Shame is about *being* a mistake — not *making* a mistake. Shame says to you, *you are a bad person* — not *you do bad things.*

Self-Messages

In a shame-based system, certain messages from yourself to yourself, self-messages for short, will trigger shame of a profound nature:

- I could have stopped it.
- It didn't happen to my sister.
- I stood by and didn't intervene.

- It felt good.
- It was the only affection I got.
- I didn't want it to stop.
- I felt like the favorite.
- My body is disgusting.
- No son of mine will be a faggot.
- I knew it was wrong.

Unpredictable Ways Shame Surfaces

Shame, too, will surface in unpredictable ways. A woman I know would literally break out in a cold sweat when she was complimented. The usual reassurances and attempts to reframe her worthiness to be complimented did not have any impact on her. The basis of the shame became clear when she reported, "I was used sexually by my father. As he fondled me, he praised me. The experience was humiliating for me, and it went on for years. Now when I am complimented, I feel tremendous anxiety. Instead of feeling good about it, I feel the shame and become panicked that my 'secret' is out."

Core of Self-Loathing

Shame is at the core of self-loathing and is very difficult to counteract. "If you knew the real me, you wouldn't even want to waste your time trying to help me."

The reality is quite different from the feelings. The reality is that the real you *is* worthy of being helped and having your needs met. The feelings of shame get in the way.

11

Anger and Rage

"My mother left me with my father, and he abused me sexually. When I saw her I would beg her to take me away from him, but she refused. I feel a lot of anger at her, but I still love her. We have a good relationship today, but I am fearful that if I ask her why she abandoned me or if I tell her how I feel about it, she will abandon me again. I can't believe she didn't know what was going on, but if I allow myself to believe that she did, I can't begin to understand how she could let that happen to me. I would prefer to stuff it than to experience those feelings again.

"I have never had a healthy intimate relationship with a man. I always set them up to leave me."

It's important to look at what this means. When she says, "I always set men up to leave me," she reveals a key element. On some level she believes that she set her mother up to leave. Even if it makes no sense, the idea that she was somehow responsible makes it tolerable to continue a relationship with her mother. It also enables her to continue in the fantasy that her mother will ultimately offer her the love the child in her continues to crave.

The idea of risking the loss of her mother again makes it improbable that her daughter will let her know the outrage that the mother permitted to happen to her. To have taken no steps to protect or save her child made the mother a willing accomplice. Until she addresses these two aspects of her past, she remains stuck in her childhood. She cannot have a healthy adult relationship with a man until some of these problems are resolved.

Dealing With Active Abuse

What about the other part? How does she deal with the active abuse? Can that be put to rest? Ironically enough this work is easier. In finding some of it pleasurable, she was reacting normally, and this knowledge is freeing.

The rage and the desire to have her father dead or out of her life forever is clear. There is nothing her father can do to right it.

This woman sees herself as someone others may like unless they get close. She believes that in getting close to her, others will discover that she is not worth being close to and that her sexual impulses are disgusting. Rather than risk this, she pushes others away.

This woman is now in group therapy. She has shared some aspects of her history, and no one has been turned off so far. The more she trusts and can share, the more able she will be to change her self-perception and overcome her need to punish herself. She will begin to release some of her anger in role playing and leave room for loving feelings to come in.

Gradually her need for her mother will become less, and she can then decide — without panic — whether or not it is in her own interest to confront her.

The other side of the rage is loss.

12

Loss

Unresolved issues of grief and loss result in depression. There is always an edge of sadness that pervades everything. The child who has suffered sexual abuse has a multitude of loss issues that need to be addressed. First, there is the loss of innocence. In a very real way, the loss of innocence is the loss of the spontaneity of childhood. Second, many have been made to act as parents and have lost their childhood in this way as well. They have experienced the loss of their personal boundaries. They could not control the use of their own bodies. They lost trust that they would be taken care of. Finally, they lost the choice of their sexual partners.

Grief

All of these losses must be mourned and acknowledged as
worthy of grief.

There is a lot to cry about. Take whatever it takes. It is not
a one-time experience.

Acceptance

With the grieving will come an acceptance. This was a
condition of my life. I was *not* responsible for what
happened: I could not change it. What happened happened.
It was real.

In the *Rubaiyat*, Omar Khayyam expressed the passage of
time in a profound way:

> *The Moving Finger writes; and, having writ,*
> *Moves on: nor all thy Piety nor Wit*
> *Shall lure it back to cancel half a Line,*
> *Nor all thy Tears wash out a word of it.*

Integration

The next part is to integrate the experience. It is a part of
what makes up who you are. Embrace all of who you are, and,
as you accept what did happen, accept yourself as a whole person. Integration is the process of putting the losses to rest. It is
a way to bury the dead. You cannot have back what is gone.

Go On With Life

Then go on with your life. Yes, you did survive where
others did not. You need not feel guilty nor question if you
are worthy of survival.

You did survive, you are surviving, and you will continue
to be. Each death can be a new beginning — if you make that
choice.

13

Enmeshment

Children growing up in a functional family will have their thoughts and feelings respected. They will have privacy in their bedroom and with their possessions. Even if a room is shared, there is an attempt made to show respect for separateness. Children are allowed privacy in the bathroom and can have a life that will include at times and exclude at times, their family.

Violation of Boundaries in Dysfunctional Homes

Children's boundaries are violated (1) when they have no rights to privacy of thoughts, feelings, or person, (2) when they are told what to think or feel, and (3) when they cannot close their bedroom or bathroom door without worrying that a parent will come in unannounced. Children are treated as possessions and not persons. Their needs are not taken into account.

Children's Purpose in Dysfunctional Homes

The violation of personal boundaries results in a situation called *covert incest* or *enmeshment.* The children's purpose is to serve the needs of the parent. If the perceived responsibility of the child is to make and keep the parent happy and the parent encourages fusion with the child, the results are:

- No individuation (sense of total separateness) of the child from the parent;
- No development of social skills among peers;
- Guilt at finding a peer sexually desirable;
- Continuous attempts to please and fulfill the role of wife or husband to the parent even as an adult, e.g., taking the parent as a date to social events;
- Idealization of the parent as love and/or sex object;
- Feelings of being idealized as love and/or sex object by parent.

If the children fail to make the world happy for the parent — and children *must* fail because a child cannot fulfill the parent but will continue to try — children cannot be happy in their own life.

Even if children marry, the incestuous bond will remain, and the children will continue to be inappropriately attentive to the parent. It is the children's responsibility to fill in the empty spaces in the life of the parent, regardless of the needs of the new family.

Children will have great difficulty in demonstrating affection to a marital partner in the bedroom. They cannot permit themselves pleasure in intimacy when the parent is denied this.

If the children choose vocations that either take them away from the parent or are not what the parent decided the children should do, the children will resist success. If the fused parent is the same sex as the child, the child will resist achieving more success than the parent.

Because of the fusion with the parent, the child will not find it unusual to feel depressed after good sex . . . if the parent did not have pleasure in his or her life, the child cannot have pleasure either.

Children's choice of a partner will be either a replica of or a reaction to their parent.

Many enmeshed people can enjoy sex as long as they are not in a committed relationship. The earlier fusion with a parent gets triggered after a commitment, such as marriage, and can be almost immediate. Other close relationships cause profound feelings of disloyalty.

A client of mine came with her lover to a lecture of mine. She introduced us later, and I was pleased that she did so. When we talked about it at our next session, she told me she was filled with anxiety about the meeting. She was afraid that I wouldn't like her lover and that she would have to make a choice between us. "Wait a minute," I said. "If you are happy, I'm pleased. There are no choices to be made."

"My mother always made me feel that if I loved someone else, I didn't love her. She hated anyone I cared about, and I always had to choose. I was isolated because I didn't have the strength not to choose her. I don't want to do that anymore. I think a part of me knew you would be different, but I was still afraid. I'm glad I took the risk."

I'm glad too.

Here are some other examples of the power of the enmeshment:

"I held my mother in my arms as she died, and as I felt her life forces ebb, I wished I could die too."

"My mother is sick. I can feel her pain as if it is my own, and I can share it with her."

A woman expressed her relationship with her father in this way: "My father wants to be enmeshed with me. He wants me to take care of him. He depends on me. He swallows me up. I struggle to maintain myself . . . If I tell him how I feel and try to get my needs met, I am afraid he will abandon me, so I swallow my feelings. It is better than being all alone."

A man shares feelings in a poem about a similar dynamic with his mother:

> *I stay connected to my mother*
> *out of guilt,*
> *which feels like love.*
> *If I let go I'll be orphaned.*
> *She doesn't meet my needs — so*
> *I feel empty inside.*
> *If I let others fill me up — I'll*
> *cut myself off from her*
> *and I'll be an orphan.*
> *So I have to be empty.*

Struggle to Individuate

The struggle to detach yourself from an enmeshed situation and to break the fusion feels like life and death. The power is tremendous: the pull seems too overwhelming to fight.

The powerful struggle to individuate leaves you with a nearly paralyzing guilt. Who you are gets caught up in the enmeshment. Your self-esteem gets confused in the role of taking care of your mother or father.

If you are not enmeshed, you will have no identity and you will be floating out there with no grounding. As one woman expressed it, "If I let go, all my insides will wash out and I'll be a puddle on the floor."

Emotionally Unavailable Parents

The result of living with emotionally unavailable parents is also abusive. Although it is hard to categorize people with this life experience as sexually abused, they identify with others who have been sexually abused.

One man reported, "I have no memory of being sexually abused, but something must have happened or I would not have been married eight times. Actually, in my case it was the reverse. My parents gave me no affection or attention. Life with them was like being in an emotional wasteland.

"The result of the deprivation was that I pressured my wives to serve my unmet needs — a chasm no woman could fill — and at the same time I had no idea how to connect with or offer nurture to them."

Not Being the "Right" Sex

For some of you the abuse took the form of your not being the "right" sex. You were supposed to be a boy. You were supposed to be a girl. You may have been dressed or named inappropriately. You may have been expected to be the daughter or son that your parents didn't have and do the boy or girl things that would have been expected of you had you been born the right sex. A girl may be naturally athletic and that can be wonderful, but to be involved in sports because that is "the only way my daddy will pay attention to me" feels very different.

With this undercurrent of parental disappointment with you, you will always feel that there is something basically wrong with you that makes you undesirable and that you cannot overcome.

Denial of Body

Other forms of sexual abuse will result in denial of body. Some results are not taking care of your body, ignoring physical problems, developing gynecological problems, having swallowing and gagging sensitivity, or wearing lots of baggy clothing, regardless of temperature or circumstance.

Sexual Functioning

Some issues are more specific to sexual functioning. People express these issues as follows:

- "Sex is disgusting and I am disgusting when I do it."
- "I can only be sexual with strangers. As soon as I care, I know I'll be betrayed."

- "I'm no good. I bring men down to my level by having sex with them. I then discard them because they're no good."
- "I panic at being touched because I am afraid that being touched will lead to abuse."
- "I can only have sex if I am the aggressor. If I am not in control, I shut down sexually."
- "I have intrusive thoughts during sex. Sometimes I even forget who I'm with."

All of these responses are understandable in light of the abuse. Knowing what the messages are is the first step toward changing them and getting your sexual self back.

14

Growing Up Gay
or Lesbian

Those who are gay or lesbian and are growing up in a dysfunctional family have all of the problems that exist for the straight person, but the problems are compounded by sexual orientation. Children in sexually abusive situations do not learn to feel good about their sexual selves. If you do not feel good about your sexual self and also desire your own sex, you are double damned.

You now have a very large secret to keep. "Things are so bad already. My secret can't get out. I have to protect this side of myself at all costs."

Not only are these feelings present but many men will report, "I know this sounds crazy, but I think my mom wanted me to be gay so she wouldn't have to compete with another woman."

A young woman very tearfully described her hunger for her mother's love. "I'm so angry. I don't think I can ever forgive her for not accepting me. She couldn't love me as I want to be loved. She made me feel disgusting. I tried so hard to please her."

The word "disgusting" is the key word. Disgusting is a shame word. It is the clue that her desire to forgive her mother is not as easily defined as she presented it. Her use of disgusting was a clue to me that she was lesbian and homophobic. She is in reality trying to forgive her mother for the wrong thing. She needs to forgive her mother for teaching her not to accept herself. She has pinned all her mother's attitudes and lack of nurture on her sexuality. She has internalized her secret and become homophobic.

As a result, she has spent many years trying to get "fixed" so that she could then gain the love and acceptance she craves. As a result, she, like so many others, has tried to get straight through therapy, heterosexual relationships, marriage, and children. This has only added to her self-hatred and increased her pain.

Abuse Occurs Regardless of Sexual Orientation

The reality is that parents who abuse their children do so regardless of the sexual orientation of their children. It is a fantasy that being straight would mean that your needs would be met. It is only a way of not holding your parents accountable for their behavior. No matter how rageful you are at them, there is the nagging sense that if you were "different" they would be different. Ironically enough, in this circumstance there is a vestige of hope that change is possible.

Some homosexuals are terrified of men because of abuse in their history or are terrified of women because of abuse in their history. Some hunger for the breast they didn't get;

others are repelled by the thought of being choked by that breast. This is true for many straight individuals as well.

Sexual Abuse Does Not Cause Homosexuality

It would be a mistake to suggest that sexual abuse causes homosexuality. Dr. Alice Moore of the Institute for Counseling and Training in West Caldwell, New Jersey, states, "I haven't found the reactions to sexual abuse in gay individuals to be any different from those in straight individuals. The essence of the person is what got damaged. Their sex preference is not relevant."

The reality is that sex preference is *not* something to be "fixed." Frankly, it is something to be comfortable with and to be celebrated.

15

Addiction

Sometimes the impact of sexual abuse will play itself out in certain compulsive behaviors. Compulsive disorders are very complicated in nature, both in what contributes to the disorder and in the ways healthy behavior change may be effected. The discussion that follows is *only* about the ways that sexual abuse is a significant contributor to compulsive disorders. It is by no means the whole picture.

Substance Abuse

Substance abuse is a form of self-medication that works. It is, therefore, not surprising that large numbers of alcoholics and drug abusers were sexually abused. Treatment centers attest to this fact, and research on runaways also indicates this.

"Don't ever tell me I was a dope to use dope. It was the only friend I had. It was the only place I could turn to to ease the pain. It was the only way I could forget. It was the only way to live through it. And if I didn't live through it, that didn't matter either."

The traditional approach to treating substance abusers is to demand abstinence. The idea is that you cannot clinically treat someone who is abusing. After all, since mind-altering substances do just that, it is not possible to know what you are treating.

For many substance abusers, abstinence as a treatment does not work. No matter how hard they try or how often they try, it does not work. It does not work because the substance serves a purpose. It has a value to the user that cannot be denied.

Some people, especially before they have been able to leave home, use the drugs in order to set up an emotional demilitarized zone. If you feel helpless and hopeless, if you know your father will be getting into your bed and you have nowhere to turn for help, reducing the pain through chemicals may seem your only way out.

Compulsive Overeating

Compulsive overeating can be one of the results of sexual abuse. The act of eating, regardless of weight gain, is experienced as self-nurture. Since nurture by another cannot be trusted, and since one is so needy, the need plays out in the eating. You do it because it makes you feel better when you eat. You do not experience it as a desire to punish yourself. The result is punishment to your body, but you don't make that connection when you do it.

Obesity serves a purpose. If you are obese, you usually feel sexually undesirable. If you are sexually undesirable, you don't have to deal with sexual advances made toward you. Obesity enables you to avoid the problem of having to deal with your sexuality.

If you are fat, you won't have to deal with your sexuality because people find fatness undesirable. It is also true that if you stay fat, you don't have to deal with the terrifying truth — as you see it — that if you were thin, you'd still be undesirable because you are not worth much.

Anorexia Nervosa

Anorexia nervosa can be another outcome of sexual abuse. Anorexia is a form of control. The loss of control over one's person that is experienced when one is sexually abused is intolerable. At least you can control what you put into your mouth.

Self-starvation in women causes cessation of the menstrual cycle and flattening of the breasts. It is seen as a fleeing from sexuality and a way of reducing the opportunity for sexual encounters.

For many people, the self-loathing is so profound that they punish themselves by denial of any nurture.

Bulimia

Bulimia is an eating disorder that combines the self-nurturing of the compulsive overeater and the control of the anorexic. It is characterized by binge eating and purging. The bulimic will eat enormous amounts of food and then throw it up or, in some cases, use laxatives to get rid of it. Essentially the sufferers of bulimia attempt to fulfill their own needs and to appear "all together" to the outside world.

As in other eating disorders, bulimics loathe themselves and feel powerless to stop the behaviors.

Self-Mutilation

This compulsive behavior results from self-loathing and disgust at one's body because of the way it has been used. It is a demonstraton of anger at self and a self-punishment. It also can come from a position of being so shut down and disconnected from one's feelings that the self-mutilation breaks through this barrier and the self-induced pain can be experienced. The feelings of the self-mutilator get distorted;

there is pleasure in feeling anything — even if it is pain — as a high can be created and re-created.

Sexual Addiction

In *Sexual Addiction* Patrick Carnes states, "A child learns from a parent how to have a relationship. When a parent is sexual with a child, the child concludes at a fundamental level that in order to have a relationship one has to be sexual. Thus, all relationships become sexualized." As this perception becomes internalized, it develops a compulsive quality because the understanding of it is not cognitive. It exists on an unconscious level. On a conscious level, the individual believes that if there is no sex, there is no relationship. Even if individuals know intellectually that their desire is an addiction, and even if they know intellectually that there is no rejection in letting a relationship develop before sexualizing it, any delay is experienced as rejection.

Since for many of you the abuse was so early that there are no words to conceptualize these feelings, it is difficult to have a conversation with yourself in order to talk yourself out of it. Since sexualizing is the only form of affection that you have understood, you are at great risk of sexualizing your relationships with your own children. You must be forever vigilant in this regard.

Since sex is the only form of affection that you understand, and since it does not provide the nurture you need, your hunger remains and is constantly in search of satisfaction.

Sex, like the other addictions, will only temporarily reduce pain. If that is your addiction, without intervention the cycle will continue to repeat itself.

Addictive Relationships

Addictive relationships are a natural for those who have been enmeshed. The child whose personal boundaries have been intruded upon does not know how to determine appropriate distance or even have an idea of what an appropriate distance might be. Enmeshment is the only relationship the child understands. The process of individuating in a healthy way is not completed, so that the longing for bonding will play itself out again and again.

If we are not as one, we are not. Thus, any attempt on the part of the other person to be separate is experienced as abandonment and creates intense desire. This desire sets up a push-pull in the relationship and maintains the high-intensity atmosphere that is the nature of addiction. Being in another addictive relationship can be a way to avoid dealing with the incestuous relationship with the parent. It is a substitution of one for the other. The addictive relationship will numb out the pain of the struggle to break the early trauma.

16

Intimate Relationships

The problems that the sexually abused persons carry with them play out in all relationships and certainly are experienced in the bedroom. Power and control issues, and trust and fear issues all come into play. They do for all couples, but they are exaggerated for those with a history of abuse.

Being hypo- or hypersexed can be a manifestation of too early sexual experience. "My body is all I have to offer," or "My body is too shameful to offer."

Flashbacks to earlier experiences are common and can cause a panic reaction or, at the very least, be a turnoff.

Fears of the Survivor

Many survivors will not tell their partners because they fear abandonment or an attitude by the partner that they are "damaged" or were in some way responsible. It would be foolish to dismiss these fears as groundless. Unfortunately, there are those who are insensitive enough to respond this way. This is a risk that may be necessary to take at the point at which the relationship becomes sexualized — if there is a sense that this will be a problem area.

Note that we are discussing a relationship, *not* a one-night stand. Relationship implies that some time has been spent getting to know and appreciate each other as people and that becoming sexually intimate is a part of this process.

Acknowledge Past Experience

It is not necessary to describe your history in graphic detail, but you should acknowledge that past experience may get in the way for a while and that patience and understanding are needed. If your potential partner does not respond in a compassionate manner, it is better to know early on so that you invest no further time in a relationship that will eventually become toxic.

This is not the time to decide that there is something wrong with you because your partner can't handle the information. Because — and this is the key — if your partner is insensitive to your needs in this aspect of your relationship, there will be insensitivity in other areas as well.

If you do not tell and you have a caring partner, your partner will begin to doubt his or her ability to please you. Your partner will begin to feel inadequate and impatient and will see himself as a lousy lover. Some people, in order to raise their sexual self-esteem, may seek other partners. The truth would ease this problem.

Share Feelings

A client of mine complained that he and his wife had not had sex for over a year. He knew she was an incest survivor, and he wanted to continue to be understanding, but he was beginning to get angry and more than a little frustrated. He felt terrible about having these feelings because he loved his wife and wanted to continue to be patient.

I told him that I'd be angry, too, if I were he, and that his feelings were appropriate. I suggested he bring it up in his therapy group and listen to the group's feedback. He was very apprehensive because several of the group members had been sexually abused as children, and he felt certain they would be outraged at his attitude.

When he took the risk, he was surprised at the response. He received support from everyone. The incest survivors suggested he confront his wife and that they approach her lack of desire as a shared problem. One woman said, "I'm not a victim of sexual abuse, but the way I punish my husband is by denying him sex. It's my most effective weapon."

That did it. He decided to share his feelings with his wife. The couple is now with a good therapist and working out their problems. It is not necessary to debate whether the denial of sex was related to the incest and was the real issue or whether the apparent problem was a smokescreen for something else. The point here is that the sexual relationship of two people needs participation by both if it is to be healthy. It requires openness and a willingness on both sides to take risks. One person cannot play both parts. It is also an important step in learning to make love and not just complying.

Lovemaking

Lovemaking involves a lot more than just being technically proficient. That comment is in no way meant to be critical of knowing the moves. But when you are building a trusting sexual relationship, the foreplay and the afterplay are critical. Remember that foreplay may take months, not minutes, and you and your partner both need to find that acceptable.

The foreplay needed includes talking, walking, holding hands, and sharing feelings, thoughts, and experiences. It may mean reading a book together. Many couples read my book *Struggle for Intimacy* and point out to each other the "stuck" places because it is easier to do that than state them out loud.

Many survivors of abuse have used alcohol and other substances to "numb themselves out." Once they have numbed out the ghosts, they are able to be sexual. As they enter recovery from chemical dependency, they are terrified of being sexual because:

- They have not been sexual sober, and it is like a new experience.
- They have fears of the past surfacing and getting in the way.
- They connected sex with chemical abuse and fear that it will trigger a relapse.

It is not unusual for a woman to be unable to reach a climax or for a man to be impotent. This, too, relates to the abuse. The statement that the female body is making is, "I will hold back some of myself so that you will not have power over me and I will not be vulnerable to you." The male body is giving a similar message. It is saying, "I will not allow myself to be entrapped and, therefore, vulnerable to you."

All these issues are resolvable over time. What is required is that you accept the fact that trust builds slowly and you can't do it alone. A relationship takes two people.

17

Post-Traumatic Stress Disorder

This disorder is understood largely as a result of work done with Vietnam veterans. Many years after experiencing combat and after appearing to function in a satisfactory way, people with Post-Traumatic Stress Disorder (PTSD) will experience symptoms of profound stress. The symptoms will be appropriate to the experience, but they were previously understood to happen at the time of the trauma. If there had been no severe reaction at that time, doctors assumed that the individual had "gotten through it" with a minimum of psychic damage. Now we know that that's not necessarily true.

It's not true for many vets and not true for the survivors of sexual abuse.

Both these vets and survivors of sexual abuse have lived through psychic and physical assaults that challenged the core of their beings. The symptoms we see with the vets are similar to those who have lived through the stress of sexual abuse.

Trigger Incident

There will be a trigger incident of major or minor proportion. It can be a perceived threat or a comment made months or years after the fact that will literally open the flood gates and render the coping mechanisms ineffectual. Symptoms will include recurrent nightmares; night terrors; fear of being alone in the dark; fear of sleeping alone; feeling separated from one's body; phobias; paranoia; fear of going crazy; fear of losing control and acting on feelings of rage; and physical symptoms such as nervousness, shaking, and breaking down of the body.

18

Developmental Triggers

When we talk about getting stuck in the trauma, not only does it mean that one relives the experience at any stressful time but also that other aspects of personality do not develop. Being stuck in the trauma is the point at which there was profound betrayal of innocence. Also, the trust that the child would use to test out and develop and grow emotionally is short-circuited.

As a result, the adult has developed unevenly. The adult role early on has accelerated one part of the maturation process, but being stuck in the trauma makes growth lag way behind in others. The amount of psychic energy needed to survive the trauma cannot be underestimated. This loss of trust can happen as the result of one event. The events around the act itself can be every bit as traumatic as the actual abuse.

Examples of Developmental Triggers

Linda, age forty-three, has been unable to connect in a serious way with either men or women. She is well-liked by both and has many opportunities, which she takes just so far and cuts off. When she was seven she was sexually molested by the older brother of a playmate. He was able to lure her because his attention made her feel special, and she was curious. She has no memory of the experience other than sitting on his lap with her pants off. She suspects rape but recalls feelings of rage and powerlessness. She has no memory of telling her mother, but she remembers her mother making a joke of it at a tea party years later.

What are the implications of this experience so many years later that prevent her from "letting it go?" What shocked her system so much that she disconnected emotionally? What lessons did she internalize that she lives out today?

She learned from the older brother that "if you make me feel special, you will violate me. And if I trust you, you will betray me."

She learned from her mother that "if I let you in on my pain and fear, you will invalidate me and mock me."

As a result of her childhood experience, when Linda begins to get close and to trust, warning signs are triggered. She experiences on an unconscious level fear of betrayal and violation. As a result, as soon as she starts to feel close, she panics and backs off. She does not yet have the freedom of choice to develop healthy close relationships.

There is no awareness on the part of others of this missing piece unless she is called on to become close. This developmental lag will become apparent once she begins to overcome her panic and fear of betrayal.

The sexual abuse itself was the least of the trauma. She is able to perform sexually — provided there is no real intimacy.

Here's another example of a developmental trigger coming into play. When Noreen's boss made a move on her, she became enraged and reported the incident. Shortly thereafter he had a heart attack, and Noreen became seriously depressed, believing she had caused it.

A fully functional adult would have behaved as she did, rebuffing the sexual advance and reporting it. But an adult would not have taken responsibility for the boss's heart attack.

As a child, Noreen learned that when she displeased her parents, they would accuse her of making them sick. The way she displeased them was when she did not comply; thus, she became compliant and buried any rights to her own needs. As long as no one got sick when she asserted herself, Noreen was fine and learned new behaviors. Had her boss not had a heart attack, this surfacing of an unresolved problem might never have been triggered.

19

Misdiagnosis

The period of latency between the time of abuse and the emergence of symptoms have caused many people to conclude erroneously that there are minimal negative consequences of sexual abuse. As a result, many adults are misdiagnosed and mistreated. Many adults will not report these experiences, minimizing their significance or relevance. It is incumbent on the therapist to ask. Any intake or initial interview that does not include this information is seriously flawed.

Clients are not responsible for knowing what is important and relevant and what isn't. The clients' responsibility is to offer whatever parts of the puzzle they can and to learn about any resistance to the process.

The counselor's awareness that sexual abuse in childhood can only be partially treated near the time of the event(s) is critical to counseling adults with this history. One never knows when something will happen — or what that something might be — that will be influenced by the childhood trauma. This is a critical insight because without the awareness and the understanding of how far-reaching the implications of sexual abuse are, the counselor will develop inappropriate types of treatment.

Many problems that relate to childhood sexual abuse show themselves in ways that mask the early history.

Masking Early History

Mary

Mary complains, "I am working two jobs. I need to quit one, but I don't seem to be able to do it. It has never been a problem before." Between the ages of nine and twelve Mary was forced to have intercourse with her father. She distrusts men and loathes her body. She has never had a serious intimate relationship with a man. Her history and fear of men are known only to her and her therapist. Others see her as a person who is at ease in the world. How does her difficulty in making a change relate to the sexual abuse?

Mary took the second job because the hours were good and she could eventually leave the first one and have more time for herself. All her arguments about needing the money are easily countered, and she doesn't accept her protests either. She continues to make up new excuses, blocking out the fact that she has already used them.

So what is it? Why the delay? What does it mean? Why the depression over something she wants and that she knows she is worth?

It is not a matter of procrastination. It is not a matter of being overwhelmed. She knows the process. It is not new to her. *It relates to the sexual abuse of her childhood.*

If she quits one job, she gains three hours a day. If she is no longer spending all her time working, she is free to do other things. If she is free to do other things, she will feel pressured to develop a social life. This is where the panic sets in and the subsequent inertia. It is such a deep-rooted fear that she is not conscious of where the panic comes from. She is terrified of developing a social life. As long as there is no time, she does not have to face her fear. The smoke screens that she sets up about finances provide a cushion between her and the real issues.

In the past this hasn't been a problem for Mary because her workaholism has eaten up her time. No longer wanting to be workaholic has put her face to face with the deeper issue. When the connections are made, tears come to her eyes and she is both relieved at the insight and sad for her ongoing struggle.

Mary's awareness that she is stuck as a result of the early sexual abuse can allow her to make the change in her life. She also can make choices about working through, in the here and now, what happened to her as a child. As Mary is able to differentiate between the past and the present, her early experiences need not permeate every aspect of her life. If her therapist did not understand the long-term impact of sexual abuse, she could easily be misdiagnosed and spend a lot of time trying to resolve the presenting problem, which is merely a manifestation of a much deeper concern.

Henry

Henry says, "I need to have some minor surgery done and I get phobic about going to the doctor." Henry was sexually abused by both his parents, who threatened to tie him down if he didn't comply. After several years of therapy, he is happily married to a woman who is supportive and understanding. Their sex life and their communication are rewarding for both of them.

How does Henry's fear of going to the doctor relate to the presenting problem? The handling of his body in ways not of his choosing brings up all Henry's early panic. He feels that he has no control over what will be done to him and that there will be dire consequences if he does not submit.

Before Henry had this insight, he reproached himself for being infantile and for not caring enough about himself to take proper care of his body. He felt foolish that his response was so powerful. When he told his friends about his fear, they told him that they, too, hated going to the doctor and knew how he felt. That made him feel isolated because he didn't identify with their feelings but didn't know why.

The phobic response and the confusion brought him back into therapy. The understanding of the connection between the early sexual abuse and the doctor phobia caused him great relief; although the idea of going to the doctor is still distasteful to Henry, he can manage it.

Many adults who have been sexually abused as children will avoid dentists and put off necessary dental work for the same reason. It is important to keep this in mind.

Two Friends

A woman in Colorado phoned me. She and a friend from Florida wanted to make an appointment to come and see me. She said that the friendship was at risk and since it was valuable to the both of them, they wanted to save it if they possibly could. She said that they were both counselors, both adult children of alcoholics, and both incest survivors.

What is the problem? The woman from Colorado said that she would call her friend and, if the friend was out, leave a message. When she received an answer, it might be months later, and the answer never related to the message that was left. This led to feelings of invalidation and anger. She resented not being heard. She then wondered if maybe she weren't making too big a deal out of it. Maybe she had unrealistic expectations of her friend. Maybe she was trying to make her be someone she wasn't.

She confronted her friend. Her friend said that she was sorry but that she would kind of go into an emotional blackout. She would appreciate receiving the call but would forget all about answering it, and when she did get around to it, she would have forgotten the content of the message. She said that she had had these kinds of blackouts before. They had cost her other friendships. Because she didn't want it to happen again, she would be willing to meet her friend in New Jersey and come to me for therapy.

I said no, I would not see them because the friendship was not the issue. If they lived in the same town, they could fight about it when it occurred and perhaps work on it together because of the frequency of the contact. She would point the distancing behavior out to her friend when it occurred, and they could come to an agreement about what to do in this event. This was not possible long distance, and it was not the real problem anyway.

The problem these two women were having is the direct result of incest. How does incest relate to not being responsive to a friend's phone call? This is clearly a very important friendship to both of them. They feel close and are very trusting. What happens to many incest survivors, however, is that feelings of trust and closeness trigger off a red flag that warns them that betrayal is just around the corner.

The conflict is so great and on such a deep level that it causes the forgetfulness. The mind can't deal with it so it buries it. It is easier to risk the loss of a friendship than to face the power of the pain of the betrayal of her parents.

My suggestion was that the woman from Florida begin to work on the issues resulting from the earlier abuse. If she doesn't, it will not be possible for her to establish healthy close relationships with lovers or with friends.

Childhood sexual abuse plays itself out in adulthood in a variety of ways. It plays itself out in ways that one would never suspect if one didn't know what to look for. It could be explained away in a variety of ways that would never get to the root of it. Misdiagnosis creates new problems that carry their own dynamics and serve to complicate and cloud over the real issues.

Presenting Problem: I Have No Problems

Sylvia had been subjected to incest by her father for a number of years and her grandfather a couple of times, and more recently had experienced date rape. A friend of hers said, "What amazes me is how well she seems to have dealt with all of this. She has made the decision not to cut off her family and, in terms of her behavior and her emotional responses to them, is able to deal appropriately with them. She sees them at intervals that are in her best interest. Sylvia holds down a good job, is careful of her personal appearance, has friends and is involved in an ongoing relationship."

I didn't buy this success story. Many people are fooled into believing that men and women recover from this level of trauma because they were too young to truly experience themselves as sexual objects. The reality is different. It is entirely possible that many men and women are able to manage or cope with the experience on the level of family of origin, that is, when dealing with their own family. I have seen that happen too often to dismiss it as a possibility. But it is impossible for someone who endured that level of sexual abuse to be unaffected by it. The question is where and how the impact is being played out.

The first place to look is in the relationship. She says she is happy in the relationship. Closer scrutiny shows that the relationship is asexual. The idea of being sexual is intolerable to her. For some reason this is also acceptable to her partner, and this fact raises many questions about the nature and limitations of the relationship. Obviously this is one place where the early trauma is being played out.

Sylvia's home is in chaos. She is upset by this and as a result does not allow anyone to visit her. This limits the degree to which others can get to know her, and she has a ready-made excuse.

If you look only at the family of origin, this client will not be helped. She will appear to have adjusted very well. In point of fact she has, given the circumstances, managed very well. But it is clear to the trained observer that the early abuse is manifesting itself in other ways.

The therapist's awareness of the link between childhood sexual abuse and adult problems is critical. Otherwise Sylvia will meet with continual failure. If chaos serves a function, no degree of educating her and developing her organizational skills is going to make a difference. In the same way, no amount of sex therapy is going to prevent her from shutting down unless she works with the connections here as well.

What is clear is that there is an impact. Child sexuality may be dormant for many until adulthood and will play itself out at that time. The clinician must always be alert to the fact that here-and-now difficulties in relationships may be the result of the early experience. Quite often there is no obvious connection; therefore, unless the clinician asks the right questions, the information will be withheld. The client may see the abuse as irrelevant, may have blocked it out, and may have amnesia of the event(s).

20

Adolescents

William R. Stender, the Chief Executive Officer of the Monmouth Chemical Dependency Treatment Center, Long Branch, New Jersey, talks about adolescents and abuse:

In a period of five years and 800 adolescent admissions ages thirteen to eighteen to our facility, we have clearly identified 60+ percent of the adolescents as being victims of overt incest and/or other sexual abuse. The incidences of covert sexual abuse probably rank as high as 80 percent, except that the covert sexual abuse is often so indefinable that it cannot easily be recognized.

Many of the kids admitted to our facility have told us that they have had multiple same-sex experiences. Some of these experiences have involved other adolescents, but others have involved adults.

We know that adolescence is a bridge to cross between childhood and adulthood. We know that one of the developmental tasks of adolescence is working on sexual identity issues.

Drug- and alcohol-induced same-sex experiences add more confusion to an already confusing period of life, and adolescents are left with even more questions about their own sexual identity. Boys and girls feel they cannot talk to peers or parents about these experiences. Unless they can discuss in treatment this level of sexual conflict and the guilt and shame associated with it, these adolescents will probably not be able to maintain abstinence from drugs or alcohol.

As we look at incest and sexual abuse issues among our adolescent population, we see some biases becoming extremely clear. These biases certainly have a great effect on treatment approaches. For example, a fifteen-year-old female who is involved sexually with a thirty-year-old male is considered to be a sex-abuse victim, and the adult is often prosecuted. On the other hand, a fifteen-year-old male who is involved sexually with a thirty-year-old female is considered to be macho and is usually praised by his father and his peers. The adult perpetrator goes unpunished.

Another important bias is that incest and sexual abuse issues are always discussed as a matter of adult to child. We need to address the kind of sexual abuse that goes on adolescent to adolescent. We know we have a sexually acting-out population in our society today. These kids have learned that sex, like the chemicals they use, feels good. Therefore it *is* good; therefore *do* it. They have not had the advantage of adult teaching and counseling about the biological, social, and moral responsibilities of their sexual behavior.

A fifteen-year-old female in a middle-class neighborhood has learned that she can get attention with sex. She has, therefore, become sexually involved with a group of adolescent males in a local park on a regular basis. She meets the boys in the park, climbs into a van, performs oral sex on one after another, and has been named by the boys, "Denise, the Blow Pig." Denise must resort to chemicals both before and after these episodes and, needless to say, Denise comes from a home where both parents are alcohol and drug addicted.

Other examples of adolescent-to-adolescent sexual abuse are found in the kinds of behavior patterns in which the male adolescent plays the role of the dominant force, and sexual activity occurs only when he wants his needs to be met.

Without intervention, these patterns certainly will carry into adulthood.

21

Sexual Abuse and AIDS

Donald McVinney, a counselor to AIDS sufferers in White Plains, New York, adds some important insights as to the effects of early sexual trauma on those individuals who have tested positive for HIV infection or already have AIDS:

Due to the social and cultural issues surrounding HIV infection and AIDS, and especially because of the routes of transmission of the HIV virus, individuals who are at risk or who have already been infected are set apart. All of the stigma associated with homosexuality, bisexuality, and use of mood-altering chemicals, especially if used intravenously, ensure that an individual's response to HIV/AIDS will be complicated. There is a perception on the part of society that these individuals have engaged in "forbidden pleasures" and, therefore, are paying the price. Individuals who have been traumatized from childhood either as a result of incest or of physical sexual abuse and molestation, and who are dealing with sexual identity issues as well as chemical dependency, are precisely the individuals who are at risk for HIV infection and who may develop AIDS. All of the above are factors that put an individual at risk.

Losses in all major life areas will be suffered by those in this society who:

- Grow up in a household with parental alcoholism;
- Are incest/rape/abuse survivors;
- Are recovering from chemical dependency;
- Are gay/lesbian.

In early childhood, the emotional effects of trauma — the feelings — get pushed down deep inside as a coping device. Individuals with this background learn to internalize good and bad feelings.

Individuals having experienced early childhood trauma, as well as those having Post-traumatic Stress Disorder are likely to:

- Manifest psychic numbing (all feelings are pushed down);
- Abuse mood-altering chemicals as a coping device;
- Have difficulty with sexuality and intimacy;
- Manifest low self-esteem and feelings of worthlessness;
- Suffer from shame and guilt (especially survivor's guilt);
- Engage in self-punishing acts and compulsive behaviors.

These traumatized individuals probably will perceive HIV infection or AIDS as justified punishment. Not only do they feel they deserve to get HIV/AIDS but a formal diagnosis of HIV or ARC/AIDS is likely to trigger in them all of the internalized feelings of shame and guilt, low self-esteem, and worthlessness.

Many people who are chemically dependent discover they are HIV positive at the time they seek treatment. For those in early recovery — when they are beginning to get in touch with primary family issues and events — a diagnosis of HIV infection seems like a fitting punishment for a less than positive life. There is an increased risk of relapse as a result.

Individuals who come from an alcoholic family system or who have experienced other forms of trauma feel like victims rather than survivors. They tend to duplicate the victim role of childhood in adulthood, resigning themselves to being victimized. This role, often played out in relationships and on the job, may be characterized as a need for self-blaming, as well as feelings of guilt, shame, embarrassment and worthlessness. HIV/AIDS becomes the actualized punishment.

Also, because those who have been traumatized often shut down their feelings and cope by the use of mood-altering chemicals and other compulsive behaviors, they are more likely to put themselves at risk for HIV infection. If HIV infection is then diagnosed, the individual from this background perceives it as justified punishment.

22

The Church

Children crave the love of parents. And, for the most part, little care is paid to how they get it. A sexual experience with a parent that is pleasurable puts the child in conflict but satisfies the need for nurture. A sexual experience with a parent that the child perceives as repulsive does not satisfy the need for nurture and puts the child into a different kind of conflict.

Honor Thy Father and Mother

The first conflict involves wanting what the child on some level knows to be wrong. It is also confusing because the idealized parent is involved in something wrong. At this stage, the child looks for and may find a way to justify the experience. The church can serve a purpose here. "Honor thy father and mother," it teaches. Somehow whatever father or mother does must be okay. And repression begins.

For the nurtured child, the conflict is exacerbated. This child is put in the position of wanting the nurture from the abusing parent. If the nurture is received, the confusion is extraordinary. If it is not received or is inconsistently received, the child is left with an empty feeling. If the child breaks the tie to the offending person, there will be an empty feeling. Particularly if that person is a parent, there will be a gaping hole where the sense of being cared for and about exists.

A spiritual relationship can help fill this space. Therefore, for many people maintaining a spiritual connection is essential. But that connection means you must honor your father and your mother. In order for children to do so, they cannot think of their parents as responsible for the sexual abuse.

Since children know it is or was wrong, and since they know it happened and the church would not tell them to honor bad people, their parents must be good people. If what happened was bad and their parents are good, then they must be bad and, therefore, responsible for whatever bad thing happened.

If children are responsible for the sexual abuse that they experienced, they do not have to reject either their parents or the church. If they are not responsible, then they are not bad. If they are good and this bad thing happened, then their parents are bad and the church is a fraud. It is too much to contemplate. Turning to the church and hearing "Honor your father and mother" scrambles the emotions even more.

It is far simpler for children to believe that they are bad and at fault for what happened than to abandon the forces in life that give nurture and definition.

This is a very profound insight and experienced at a very deep emotional level. It is not unusual for men or women with this history to believe intellectually whatever they are told about having no blame for the abuse but to make no progress emotionally.

They will come into treatment for relationship issues. I worked with a delightful young woman who was soaring in her career and appreciated by those with whom she came in contact. What brought her to treatment was that, in the past, when she was at a job long enough for people to want to get to know her better, she would become extremely anxious. The anxiety had become great enough in the past for her to leave jobs that she loved on at least two occasions.

"What's wrong with me?" she cried. "I like people. I want to make friends, but I am terrified that if they get to know what I am really like, they won't want to know me anymore.

"As soon as the work situation becomes somewhat social, I start to panic. I make up excuses why I can't see my co-workers outside of the office; when those excuses are all worn out, either they leave me alone and I feel isolated and depressed or they don't give up and I panic and leave the job. I hate this in myself and don't want to be like this anymore."

The anguish of this woman ran deep. There is no evidence in the real world that she is not a super human being. The conflict exists elsewhere. This woman was physically and sexually abused by both her parents for much of her childhood. Her parents were also profoundly religious — in this case, Roman Catholic — and she was drawn to the church.

When we talked about her parents and the abuse, she told me how difficult a child she was and that she deserved the frequent beatings they gave her. When I questioned that perception, she decided that maybe her memories were incorrect because her parents were good people. Whatever happened had to be her fault. Even if she was only three and three-year-olds are too young to cause abuse, in her case it was different. If she had not been born, everything would have been fine. And she didn't make up that idea: her parents had told her that many times. After all, they had to know because they were her parents and they didn't say that to the other kids.

As an adult, she would enter a monastery whenever an event would trigger emotional pain. She decided at one point to become a nun but left the convent after a year. Her attachment to the cloistered life remained, and periodically when she felt lonely or stressed, she would return to the cloister. Since this was not her answer, either, she would stay for a while and then reenter the secular world. She felt she belonged nowhere.

The treatment plan had to take all these factors into account; ideas that make no sense in the world of reason — like a three-year-old causing her own abuse — serve a purpose. To dismiss these ideas as meaningless is to lose the trust of the client.

Why does an intelligent sensitive woman reject any attempt to deny that she caused her own pain? As intolerable as the pain is when she connects with it, she is cut off from her family if she gives up responsibility. She could not be connected to people who could willfully harm her. Furthermore, she is cut off from the church: she could not follow the tenets of a religion that told her to honor her parents if they were bad people.

Rather than be adrift and alone on this planet without an anchor of any sort, she'll explain away her history. After all, her parents had difficult childhoods, too, and don't we all behave in accordance with our history? You have to understand where they're coming from. You can't be a good Christian if you have no compassion and can't turn the other cheek.

In order for you to begin the healing process, it is essential for you to acknowledge that you cannot jump from abuse to understanding and resolve the feelings of alienation and shame. It simply isn't possible. Peace does come with compassion and understanding, but true compassion and understanding exist only when self-forgiveness and resolution of anger have been processed.

How can you heal from the abuse when the price of the healing means abandoning both your family and your church? How can you heal when the price of healing is that you must be all alone in a world you are not deeply connected to? How can you take that awesome risk? Can it possibly be worth it? Is there a way to manage it?

The answer is *yes.* There is a way to manage it, fully respecting the profound nature of the commitment. There is a process involved. You need to understand fully the process and the steps that are involved. You must then commit to working through all of the steps. None can be skipped, and each may be done more than once. When you start to panic — and you will — read through the steps that follow the step where you are. The answer to your fear should be contained in the steps that are explained in the chapter entitled "The Healing" (p. 105).

A fact that you *must* recognize and accept is that your understanding of the position of the church is a distortion. It is very limited in scope and leaves out your sense of yourself as having value as a creature of God. As a result you are not able to avail yourself of the help necessary to overcome the abuse that you suffered.

Religious Problems to Getting Help

Father James Mahoney of the Paterson Archdiocese, Paterson, New Jersey, has offered the following thoughts:

Some persons who have suffered from sexual abuse are reluctant to obtain professional help due to their religious background. Usually, the problem works like this: the commandments tell us to honor our father and mother. If we have been abused sexually or physically by our parents, then it seems to be disloyal to them to seek professional help.

When persons are in this quandary, it seems that they have only remembered part of the message in their religious upbringing. Far too many persons have lost sight of the fact that we are called upon to love God, our neighbor, and ourself. An unhealthy and negative approach to religion has given some the idea that taking care of oneself is actually selfish. This is simply a false understanding of religion.

Religion involves a recognition that we are called upon to love God, our neighbor, and ourself.

Since God is the Creator, constant teaching in the Jewish and Christian traditions is that each person experiences the life and love of God. We are created by God; therefore, there is a strong moral need to take care of ourselves since we are connected with the life and love of God.

For people who have been abused physically or sexually by their parents, the need to take care of themselves and to seek professional help has nothing at all to do with honoring or not honoring their parents. It is a simple recognition that, if we were put here by God, we must do everything we can to take care of ourselves.

Religion is also about the righting of wrongs, resisting evil, and overcoming conditions that are sinful. Persons who have been sexually or physically abused deserve, out of love of God, to be helped. Religious training, rather than causing reluctance to seek help, should be used to remind persons of this obligation we have to take care of ourselves. Taking care of ourselves is an important way to honor God.

The commandments to love God, our neighbor, and ourself are the greatest commandments we can ever follow. Helping yourself is not selfish. Getting help for yourself is not disloyal. It is the best thing to do because God loves you. If you have been told that getting help goes against the love of God and the commandments, then you have received some bad advice. The best advice is to love God, love your neighbor, and be good to yourself. That is moral advice, religious advice, and the most helpful advice you can follow.

A Jewish Perspective

Rabbi Perry Raphael Rank of Springfield, New Jersey, offers the following perspective:

If every copy of the Bible suddenly disappeared and a group of Sunday School children were assigned the task of reconstructing it, the new version would probably begin: "Honor your father and your mother . . ." It's one of those rules that just about everyone knows. Of course, when it comes to famous rules, it helps to be one of the Ten Commandments (check it out: Exodus 20:12), but there is yet another reason for this particular commandment's fame.

Of all the many rules in the Torah (that's the Hebrew term for the Five Books of Moses), the rule of Parental Honor is one of only two for which fulfillment brings reward — *Honor your father and your mother, that you may long endure on the land which the Lord your God is giving you.* Linking reward with commandment was the Torah's way of emphasizing the precept. The honor due parents is thus a commandment given special consideration.

Unfortunately, the Torah does not let on as to exactly what it means by "honor." Later Tradition developed in such a way as to explain the term the way anyone — given sound mind, a pencil, and pad of paper — might explain it. Tradition mandated that children be prepared to provide food, clothing, and shelter if needed; avoid reprimands; adhere to absolute civility during the course of conversation; and accommodate the parent in requests made.

But Tradition also recognized the problem in a parent's request that entails the child's violation of another Torah commandment. For example, what if a parent asks his or her child to steal from a competitor in business or lie under oath during court proceedings? Such a request would seem to place the child in an ugly dilemma. Obey the parent and the Torah is violated; deny the parent's request and the Torah is also violated.

The scenario of such a conflict darkens when a parent requests or demands sexual favors of the child. According to the Torah, such a request or demand is completely illegal. Sexual relations between father and daughter are prohibited in Leviticus 18:17; between mother and son in Leviticus 18:7. An incestuous parent exploits the child's legitimate need for affection by trespassing a sacred boundary into the realm of forbidden sexuality. The child is cornered into a no-win situation. Submit to the parent and one's body, let alone the Torah, is violated; stand by the Torah's principles, and the child must face the unjustified wrath of the parent.

The rabbis understood the dilemma and proposed a solution.

Although the Torah explicity states that parents must be honored, the Torah is equally clear on honoring another, decidedly superior parent: God. If ever two competing demands arose between the biological parent and God, it was the will of the divine Parent that took precedence. In this way, the rabbis taught that children can never be placed in the ugly dilemma mentioned earlier. Once a parent's demand constitutes a violation of Torah, the Torah here understood as the will of God, the child need no longer fear disobeying the parent. To honor God comes first; to disobey the parent, in such a case, would be a virtue.

Moreover, violation of the body is easily regarded by Jewish tradition as an affront to God. How so? That, in fact, is one of the interpretations of Genesis 1:27, an aggressively thought-provoking verse: *And God created man in His image, in the image of God He created him; male and female He created them.* In other words, to violate man is to violate God. On some metaphysical level, a sexually abusive parent is striking the face of God.

All this should come as no surprise. Jewish tradition has always perceived the human being as part divine. Call it what you will — the soul or, as we might say in Hebrew, the *n'shamah* — there is something within us that is godly. We are consequently obligated to protect ourselves, even from parents. There is a limit on the extent to which we honor or obey them. As the Talmud states (Kiddushin 30b), three are responsible for the creation of Man: a father, a mother, and God. And of those three, we owe no parent greater honor than the Father/Mother of all humanity and indeed, of the universe itself.

A Different Problem

Among fundamentalist believers, the injunction to honor one's parents is primary. If this is the belief, then the counseling process, at some stages, will be in direct conflict. That being the case, making peace with the past and not repeating it in the future present a very different problem. Those of you who are in this dilemma need to begin to dialogue with each other in order to find a compatible resolution.

23

Forgiveness

Do I have to forgive my abuser? Do I have to give up loving my parents? After all, they were sick, too; they didn't *mean* to hurt me.

Whether or not you forgive or feel compassion is an individual choice. If your parents were the abusers, you may continue to have the need to feel connected in some way, regardless of whether or not you want to feel that way.

Dealing With Rage

Dealing with your rage is a component of the healing process. Rage is the main block to forgiveness. It is also an appropriate response to what happened to you.

You may need help getting to this feeling because your anger has been repressed. You were unable to assert yourself in your own behalf and need to be able to do so in order to give up the victim role.

You need to express and slowly work through the feelings of rage. Getting stuck in the rage is not good for you. It generalizes and leaves you with a hostile attitude toward life and means others will be reluctant to draw close to you.

If you have a need to love the perpetrator, you still have to go through the rage process in order to feel true compassion or to forgive. If you don't, your forgiveness will only be an intellectual understanding. Intellectual understanding does *not* mean you have worked through the feelings you need to in order to heal. Forgiving too early leaves you in the victim role.

What happened to you will *never* be okay. The awareness of how disturbed someone who abuses children is, may be a part of your spiritual recovery.

Choices

Forgiveness is *not* an obligation. Compassion for and understanding of the perpetrator's illness are *not* an obligation. They are choices. Make whatever choice helps you feel better about yourself.

24

The Healing

The 12 Steps of AA have been translated for use by many self-help groups. No cluster of principles has been found to be more useful in the healing process. For that reason those of you who have developed compulsive or addictive behaviors are encouraged to seek out the appropriate self-help group as a step in your journey toward wholeness. It is also my belief that working with a therapist is a useful part of the healing process.

Self-help and self-help groups are designed to offer support and encouragement. They are a place to share what steps others have taken that have helped them to heal. The nurture and identification are wonderful. However, self-help groups should not be a return to the trauma but ways to behave healthfully in the here and now.

All of this, though therapeutic, is not therapy. To decide to enlist the aid of a professional does *not* mean you are sicker than those who choose to go it alone. What it does mean is that you avail yourself of someone's training to gain insight into the meanings you have put to your life experience.

The Road to Healing

In order to start on the road to healing, you have to admit that you were a victim. You have to admit you were powerless to change what happened. You had and have no responsibility for the event(s) that took place. That is the first part.

Express What Happened

One of the ways to begin to make these admissions is to express what happened. There are reasons why it is important to tell your story: writing it down and/or saying it out loud puts the experience outside yourself. Telling your story helps you begin the process of separating from the abuse and not carrying it around inside of you. Externalizing it also begins to make it more manageable. You can look at what is real and begin to sort it out.

Admit That Life Is Unmanageable

The other part of this step is to admit that your life is unmanageable. It is unmanageable because the feelings that you are trying to control leave you out of control. The struggle to keep the fears, the pain, and the rage safely hidden leave you feeling overwhelmed. Keeping the secret and behaving "as if" is exhausting. The coping mechanisms are no longer working. It is simply too big a task. It is time to admit that your life is unmanageable.

Admit to Being Victimized and to Needing Help

Admit that you were victimized and that you cannot overcome the effects all by yourself. Up until now you have taken responsibility both for what happened to you and for recovering from it. You are now saying you did not cause it nor can you cure it. It is not difficult to understand why many of you have held the secret for this long.

Although the content of particular anecdotes varies from person to person, the response to the question, "Why did you keep it to yourself?" is always the same. "There was no one to tell. Telling would only make it worse."

"Telling would make it real."

"Maybe I'm making it up."

"I wouldn't be believed."

"I would be blamed."

"My father would get so upset I'd end up taking care of him."

"Nothing would change."

"I couldn't trust a stranger."

"The overwhelming feelings are of terror and helplessness."

The reality is that without the appropriate intervention, you would have realized your worst fears. It is terrible to have to admit this, but just telling creates a new set of problems that are also excruciatingly painful. The abandonment that you felt not only by the perpetrator but by disbelieving family members who do not want the apple cart upset would have been an additional trauma. The decision to "push it down" is not difficult to understand.

When you are an adult, something may occur that will act as a trigger. The repression will no longer be useful. The purpose that it once served will no longer be operant, and the defense will deter growth. Once the disclosure is made, many symptoms will surface that previously were kept under wraps. When the information is recalled, the memories will be vivid and arouse very intense feeling.

You will return to the trauma and the emotional impact of the enormity of that experience. The impact may be far greater than the coping mechanism allowed at the time of the experience. Previously repressed memories may start to emerge. Some may surface as memories, some as dreams, and some perhaps even as hallucinations. There may be recurrent nightmares. There also may be a compulsive telling just as there was a compulsive nontelling. Stress-related physical problems may also surface. All of these developments are very powerful. The power of the pain and the subsequent fear is *not* a sign that you are going crazy. These feelings that explode "out of nowhere" are not a sign that you have lost it. The subsequent confusion does not mean that you are going crazy. It is just the opposite. It is a sign that the healing process is beginning. It is the start of recovery and time to find appropriate help. You need not do it alone.

Exposure of "The Secret"

The first person to whom you need to expose the secret is yourself. Regardless of how horrible an experience is, it is all the more horrible if it is contained within. Denial, the pushing down of thoughts and feelings, or dismissal does not make an experience more manageable in the long run. Taking the experience and putting it outside of yourself so that it can be examined, discussed, explored, and controlled is necessary to getting past it.

Write About What Happened

Take paper and pencil and write down the story of what happened to you. Do it much the same way the recovering person does in Alcoholics Anonymous. Write about every aspect of the experience. Answer questions of who, what, when, where, and how often. It is important to include all the details that you can think of. Some of you may have great recall of the minutest details, and it is important to include them.

Write About Feelings

Others may "know" that something happened but not be able to recall any particular event. That is okay too. Just put down what your feelings are, the ways in which you identify with sexual abuse victims — whatever fragments of memory you have, regardless of whether or not you are absolutely certain that it did. The order doesn't matter; the spelling doesn't matter; there is no right way or no wrong way. It just needs to be put down — whatever it is.

Write down your feelings as you write about your experience(s). What happened to you is no more important than how you feel about it. No experience is too big or too little and no feeling too bizarre to be expressed. Confusion is as valid a response as anything else.

Share These Notes

Share these notes with another, carefully selected person. My preference is that you share them with a therapist — one who understands how to help sexual abuse victims. If one is not available to you or you choose not to seek the help of a professional at this time, share your notes with a friend who has also been sexually abused. The identification is important because your feelings will be validated and your questions will be familiar. Sharing with someone who cares about you but has not had the experience will not have the result you want and may not be useful to you. The other person may care, but caring does not guarantee real understanding.

Steps to Take in the Recovery Process

Healing is a process that involves the whole person. Just looking at the sexual abuse in isolation will not do it. The goal is to improve the quality of your entire life.

Certainly, overcoming the trauma of sexual abuse can be the initial focus, but it cannot end there. The recovery process involves some steps. The steps presented do not have to be done in the order in which they are listed (and they will be returned to more than once):

1. Take a look at what happened and understand the meaning that the experience took on in your life.
2. Become aware of what is going on with you as a result of the past and how it influences you in the present.
3. Address all the feelings involved and commit yourself to working through them. These feelings include the fears, the sense of loss and betrayal, and the rage. All these responses need be brought to the surface and faced.

4. Insight is not enough. Action must be taken. You need to make decisions about what you want to do with your life and develop a plan for doing it.
5. Recognize what blocks are in the way of your accomplishing these goals.
6. Work on overcoming these blocks.
7. Take the action steps.

Developing a New History

Taking action will help in the development of a new history. It will then become a history where you are in charge of your life and can make decisions that are in your best interest. You are no longer the victim. Not only have you survived, but you can feel good about being you. The essence of you belongs to you, and no one can abuse that special part of what makes up that special person who is you.

Going through this process will give you a sense of serenity. You will have exposed your secret and put some of the pain and anger outside of you. That process will leave room, if you choose, for love of a Higher Power and for love of yourself and your fellow human beings.

You can now be there for others and help them travel this journey of growth and celebration as whole persons worthy of offering love and being treated in a loving way.

We do not exist without purpose. All of our life experiences help bring us closer to realizing that purpose.

The abuse you overcame can give further meaning to your life in your service to others and in your acceptance of self. The loss you experienced needs to be acknowledged, grieved over, accepted, and integrated as a part of who you are.

Be grateful that you survived and use that awareness to live a more enriched life.

25

A Word to
Friends and Lovers

The results of sexual abuse affect not only the people who have lived the experience but also the people who care for them. The closer the connection, the greater the impact. This book would not be complete if it did not address itself to those who care. It is crucial to work through the pain of abuse on an individual basis, as well as to address the ways in which friendships and love relationships are made more difficult. Since none of us lives in a vacuum, it is not possible to define and work on the areas that involve interaction with others without the active, willing participation of those who care. Just caring is not enough. Having an idea of the pitfalls and how to participate in overcoming them can make for a very fulfilling relationship. Just caring does not do it. There are specific things that can make a difference.

Become Educated

Read books on the subject of sexual abuse to better educate yourself as to what the life experience has been. Try to read with an eye toward better understanding what your friend or lover experiences. (Recommended books are noted with an asterisk in the bibliography, p. 123.)

Accept emotionally, as well as intellectually, the reality that children are not responsible for the abuse they suffered, regardless of the circumstances and regardless of their behavior. There is no way the victim is responsible. If any part of you cánnot believe this fact, talk to others who can help you believe it. If you are unable to accept the innocence of the victim, it is important for you to know that you cannot be an appropriate friend or lover for someone with this history. No matter how hard you try to hide these feelings, they will be known on some level and will add to the feelings of guilt and shame already carried by the abused person.

"How could you?" and "Why didn't you . . . ?" may be questions you need to ask, but all they say is that you really don't understand. I remember receiving a phone call from a man who had just learned that his girlfriend had been raped. He was desperate because she had a good working knowledge of karate, was close to a black belt, and yet had "let" this happen to her. He was tortured because he couldn't let go of the feeling that somehow she had wanted it, and he didn't want to go near her. He didn't want to continue in this belief or he wouldn't have called.

As we talked and I tried to explain to him what happens in these circumstances, he continued to say, "Yeh, but . . . yeh, but." Then I began to learn about him. He told me that he had been in combat in Vietnam.

"Were you ever really scared?" I asked.

"Oh, yes."

"Were you ever so scared that you couldn't move — that you were frozen to the spot?"

"Not only that," he said, "I found out the true meaning of the expression, 'I was so scared I shit in my pants.' "

"Really," I said. "And with all your experience and military training and weapons you would still experience such a level of terror that you were immobile?"

"I get it," he said. "Thank you."

Disclosure

Your friend or lover may not have told you about her past, and you may feel that you had a right to know. Recognize that the anger you may feel because this secret was kept from you may be unjustified. Your friend or lover is afraid that once you know, you will find her disgusting and want to walk away. Even if she wants to tell, her vocal cords won't work. There is no way that this information does not become a variable in the relationship. "It won't make any difference in the way I feel about you," is sheer nonsense.

Disclosure may elicit feelings of great sorrow or pity for your friend. This is probably the last way that she wants you to feel.

You may become overprotective and careful of what you say, treating your friend as if she were an invalid.

Your friend or lover may be fearful that you will see her as damaged and want to "fix" her.

You may want to kill the perpetrator and he may still be seeking the love and/or approval of that person especially if the perpetrator is a parent.

You will have to act as if you don't know when you are around your friend's family, if that is his wish.

Your friend or lover is consumed with panic at sharing the secret and the negative ways that she is imagining you will react. There is no room for the awareness that you will feel a certain relief that problems that you thought were your fault had nothing to do with you.

Be careful not to say things like, "I understand how you feel," if you have not had a similar experience. Validate your friend's feelings: "I would be angry too." "The feelings of betrayal must be intense." "Thank you for trusting me enough to tell me. Is there a way I can help?"

Be careful not to minimize the event, even if your friend does not recall the actual abuse. Statements like, "That was then and this is now. It's time to leave that behind and go on with your life," though well intentioned, are most insensitive. If he could have put it to rest and gone on just like that and not be affected he would have. No one wants to continue suffering the effects of abuse.

Trust

Recognize that trust will build slowly, and you will have to be very patient in this regard. Even if you are a very trustworthy person and even if you give your friend nothing to question, the questions will persist. If you are late, if you have a quarrel, if you meet with another friend, or if you make a careless remark — there may be a powerful response. It may have been something you had no control over, but it will set off fears of deceit, betrayal, and abandonment. You need to be aware of it. Constant reassurance will be helpful, but since the lack of trust is not something you initiated, you will not be able to resolve it wholly. You may become someone to be trusted, but it will take time.

Sexual Relationships

The sexual relationship may present one or more problems:

1. Your lover may have no interest in sex or may be unable to enjoy it.
2. Your lover may believe that all he has to offer is his body and feel rejected if you are not always ready to be physical.
3. Your lover may find her body disgusting, and hide it or the reverse — flaunt it and be seductive with others — even if there is no intent

to follow through or consciousness of the behavior.

4. Your lover may flash back on the abuse during intimate moments and become turned off.

5. You may believe that if you were more adequate as a lover, these problems would not exist. Not true.

6. You will need to take time to be comfortable with each other and pay very special attention to being affectionate and loving as you are being sexual.

Maintaining a Relationship

Your friend or lover may be convinced that he is worthless as a human being — certainly not worthy of being cared for by you — and may move to break off the relationship before you do so as not to experience your abandonment. This will occur more often when things are going well than when they are going badly. You will have to be continually encouraging in order for your lover to stay, but there is that risk of his leaving. Bear in mind that much sexual abuse was perpetrated by someone who was loved and trusted, and feelings of love and trust can trigger panic. Encourage your friend or lover to fight it out if this occurs rather than to flee. If fleeing has been a pattern, then you can know in advance. You will also have to decide if you are willing to take the risk. Remember, you have feelings and needs, too.

Easing Rage or Fear

Your friend or lover may become fearful or angry when you least expect it, and those feelings may seem to come out of nowhere. It is important to be clear when the degree of anger is displaced and not to buy into it. "Yes, I told an off-color joke and I'm sorry if it upset you. But it was not my intent to insult you or mock you. That is simply not me!"

Try to appease the fears. "I will walk you to your door." "Can I come with you to the doctor?" "Is there a way I can help make it easier for you?" "No, you are not stupid to be afraid."

Although you cannot "fix" the rage or the fear, you may be able to help ease it.

Accompany Victim to Therapy

Therapy can be very beneficial to individuals who have been abused, and your lover may decide to seek help. Be available to go with him or her. It will then become clearer as to how the early experiences impact on your relationship and how the two of you can learn ways to resolve the difficulties.

Don't Neglect Yourself

Above all, don't neglect yourself. If you devote yourself entirely to the well-being of someone else, you will eventually begin to resent it. You will feel guilty because you resent someone who did not bring her suffering upon herself, but you will begin to resent her, regardless. The person that you have devoted yourself to will be grateful at first, but if she grows stronger, your tireless devotion will feel like an anchor. You will find yourself in an untenable position. You will feel unappreciated and angry. You may want to leave the relationship, but how can you walk away from someone who is wounded and maintain your self-respect? How can you stay with someone who can't come to grips with her history and not have it drain you and become destructive to your well-being?

If you come from a dysfunctional family where it was your job to take care of everyone, you will get sucked in and play out your childhood role once again. It will not work this time, either, but you will once again get sucked deeper into your fantasy of being able to fix. As a result you will continue to lose yourself and end up orbiting around your partner.

Establish Ground Rules for a Relationship

You need to be aware of your needs and desires. It is important for you to be patient, but you need to establish ground rules if the relationship is going to work. If you know what your partner needs from you, and your partner knows what you need, then you can work toward meeting those needs and working out the problems that get in the way. Either you can do it as a couple or you can't. As you attempt to work out the problems, you need to set up goals and a time frame to resolve your problems as a couple. The other part of the ground rule is that if you both don't feel that you are progressing, go together to a counselor.

If you are not willing to go for help, or your partner is not willing to go for help, you may have to consider carefully if the relationship is viable.

Remember, you did not cause the abuse nor can you cure it. You can be part of the recovery process. Problems that interfere with intimacy have shared as well as individual aspects. You can work on these aspects as a couple if both of you are committed to doing so. You will not be issue-free either, and couples work on shared problems. The goal is not to "fix" the sick but to work on health.

26

Intervention, Prevention, and Treatment

Any discussion of abuse must include serious consideration of ways to prevent, intervene, and treat. These aspects must be explored in an urgent manner.

Prevention

Prevention is obviously the most critical. There are definite steps to be taken in this regard.

The School and the Community

The schools in their health programs from the earliest years onward *must* address (1) the right to privacy of one's

119

body, (2) the nature of touching that is okay, (3) the nature of touching that is not okay, (4) the way to say no, and (5) the action to be taken. As an example, the simple but direct public service announcements and school reinforcement about not accepting rides from strangers make a positive impact on children. Some communities are resistent to the school playing this role in the lives of their children. I do not have much patience for this. School systems must take risks, and even in communities where there is risk in terms of funding, a stand must be taken. Any adult who does not actively take a position in this regard is an accessory. There is no middle ground.

For some small children the prevention effort also will provide a climate for intervention because children who are being abused at the time of this education may appear confused, distant, or sorrowful, or may simply go to sleep. The further point here is that people imparting these lessons ought to have some training in how to identify children who are or who have been sexually abused.

Mass Media

The other strategy for prevention is use of the mass media in the teaching role. Children's programming should include pointers on how to say no and on how to distinguish between acceptable and unacceptable touching. There should also be a hotline for children to call if they need help.

Intervention and Treatment

Report Suspected Child Abuse

In New Jersey the Division of Youth and Family Services is legally mandated to respond to reports of suspected child sexual abuse within twenty-four hours. Other states have other names for child protective agencies, but the procedure is the same. Mental health professionals are required by law to report such suspicions. Private citizens should report any question about abuse as well. There is no requirement that you identify yourself. Teachers and counselors need to be taught what to look for and, when they have suspicions, to report them.

Children need advocates. Adults who refuse to be involved help perpetuate the problem. The impact of the sexual abuse varies: some children *appear* to be minimally affected; others are profoundly affected. All are affected and in need of assistance. In fact, all family members are affected and in need of assistance.

Treatment and Follow-Up

Any treatment that is to be effective not only *must* address the current experience but also include a five-, ten-, and fifteen-year follow-up. Symptoms of this experience may remain dormant for a long time. However, we know a circumstance can arise that triggers them. We know that these triggers may occur at any time. If we are not aware that the effects of sexual abuse can manifest themselves at later times in different forms, the struggle to overcome our childhood sexual trauma will be misdiagnosed and we will not find appropriate treatment.

Our awareness of the problems of sexual abuse can help us heal our sexual selves and lead full and healthy lives.

Bibliography

* Allen, Charlotte Vale. *Daddy's Girl.* New York: Berkley Books, 1984.

* Carnes, Patrick. *Out of the Shadows.* Minneapolis, MN: CompCare Pub., 1983.

* Donaldson, MaryAnn. *Incest Years After — Putting the Pain to Rest.* Fargo, ND: Village Family Service Center, 1983.

* Forward, Susan. *Betrayal of Innocence.* New York: Penguin Books, 1979.

Gelinas, Denise J. *Psychiatry,* vol. 46, Springfield, MA: Dept. of Psychiatry — Incest Treatment Program, Baystate Medical Center, Nov. 1983.

* Gornick, Vivian. *Fierce Attachments.* New York: Simon and Schuster, 1988.

* Janssen, Martha. *The Silent Scream.* Philadelphia, PA: Fortress Press, 1983.

Kerach, Judith A. "Incest as a Treatment Issue for Alcoholic Women." *Alcoholism Treatment Quarterly.* 1986. 3 no. 1:1-30.

King, Elayne J. "Analysis of Somatic Dysfunction in Adult Survivors of Father-Daughter Incest." Unpublished dissertation, Hofstra University, NY, 1985.

Meyer, Adele. *Incest: A Treatment Manual for Therapy with Victims, Spouses and Offenders.* Holmes Beach, FL: Learning Publications, 1983.

Sgior, Suzanne M. *Handbook of Clinical Intervention in Child Sexual Abuse.* Lexington, MA: Lexington Books, 1982.

---

* Recommended books to read on the subject of sexual abuse.

Other Books By . . .

HEALTH COMMUNICATIONS, INC.

Enterprise Center
3201 Southwest 15th Street
Deerfield Beach, FL 33442
Phone: 800-851-9100

ADULT CHILDREN OF ALCOHOLICS
Janet Woititz
Over a year on The New York Times Best Seller list,this book is the primer on Adult Children of Alcoholics.

ISBN 0-932194-15-X   **$6.95**

STRUGGLE FOR INTIMACY
Janet Woititz
Another best seller, this book gives insightful advice on learning to love more fully.

ISBN 0-932194-25-7   **$6.95**

DAILY AFFIRMATIONS: For Adult Children of Alcoholics
Rokelle Lerner
These positive affirmations for every day of the year paint a mental picture of your life as you choose it to be.

ISBN 0-932194-27-3   **$6.95**

CHOICEMAKING: For Co-dependents, Adult Children and Spirituality Seekers — Sharon Wegscheider-Cruse
This useful book defines the problems and solves them in a positive way.

ISBN 0-932194-26-5   **$9.95**

LEARNING TO LOVE YOURSELF: Finding Your Self-Worth
Sharon Wegscheider-Cruse
"Self-worth is a choice, not a birthright", says the author as she shows us how we can choose positive self-esteem.

ISBN 0-932194-39-7   **$7.95**

LET GO AND GROW: Recovery for Adult Children
Robert Ackerman
An in-depth study of the different characteristics of adult children of alcoholics with guidelines for recovery.

ISBN 0-932194-51-6   **$8.95**

LOST IN THE SHUFFLE: The Co-dependent Reality
Robert Subby
A look at the unreal rules the co-dependent lives by and the way out of the dis-eased reality.

ISBN 0-932194-45-1   **$8.95**

New Books . . .
from Health Communications

BRADSHAW ON: THE FAMILY: A Revolutionary Way of Self-Discovery
John Bradshaw
The host of the nationally televised series of the same name shows us how families can be healed and we as individuals can realize our full potential.
ISBN 0-932194-54-0 $9.95

HEALING THE CHILD WITHIN: Discovery and recovery for Adult Children of Dysfunctional Families — Charles Whitfield
Dr. Whitfield defines, describes and discovers how we can reach our Child Within to heal and nurture our woundedness.
ISBN 0-932194-40-0 $8.95

WHISKY'S SONG: An Explicit Story of Surviving in an Alcoholic Home
Mitzi Chandler
A beautiful but brutal story of growing up where violence and neglect are everyday occurrences conveys a positive message of survival and love.
ISBN 0-932194-42-7 $6.95

New Books on Spiritual Recovery . . .
from Health Communications

THE JOURNEY WITHIN: A Spiritual Path to Recovery
Ruth Fishel
This book will lead you from your dysfunctional beginnings to the place within where renewal occurs.
ISBN 0-932194-41-9 $8.95

LEARNING TO LIVE IN THE NOW: 6-Week Personal Plan To Recovery
Ruth Fishel
The author gently introduces you to the valuable healing tools of meditation, positive creative visualization and affirmations.
ISBN 0-932194-62-1 $7.95

GENESIS: Spirituality in Recovery for Co-dependents
by Julie D. Bowden and Herbert L. Gravitz
A self-help spiritual program for adult children of trauma, an in-depth look at "turning it over" and "letting go".
ISBN 0-932194-56-7 $6.95

GIFTS FOR PERSONAL GROWTH AND RECOVERY
Wayne Kritsberg
Gifts for healing which include journal writing, breathing, positioning and meditation.
ISBN 0-932194-60-5 $6.95

Books from . . .
Health Communications

THIRTY-TWO ELEPHANT REMINDERS: A Book of Healthy Rules
Mary M. McKee
Concise advice by 32 wise elephants whose wit and good humor will also
be appearing in a 12-step calendar and greeting cards.
ISBN 0-932194-59-1 $3.95

BREAKING THE CYCLE OF ADDICTION: For Adult Children of Alcoholics
Patricia O'Gorman and Philip Oliver-Diaz
For parents who were raised in addicted families, this guide teaches you
about Breaking the Cycle of Addiction from *your* parents to your children.
Must reading for any parent.
ISBN 0-932194-37-0 $8.95

AFTER THE TEARS: Reclaiming The Personal Losses of Childhood
Jane Middelton-Moz and Lorie Dwinnel
Your lost childhood must be grieved in order for you to recapture your
self-worth and enjoyment of life. This book will show you how.
ISBN 0-932194-36-2 $7.95

ADULT CHILDREN OF ALCOHOLICS SYNDROME: From Discovery to Recovery
Wayne Kritsberg
Through the Family Integration System and foundations for healing the
wounds of an alcoholic-influenced childhood are laid in this important
book.
ISBN 0-932194-30-3 $7.95

OTHERWISE PERFECT: People and Their Problems with Weight
Mary S. Stuart and Lynnzy Orr
This book deals with all the varieties of eating disorders, from anorexia to
obesity, and how to cope sensibly and successfully.
ISBN 0-932194-57-5 $7.95

Orders must be prepaid by check, money order, MasterCard or Visa.
Purchase orders from agencies accepted (attach P.O. documentation)
for billing. Net 30 days.
Minimum shipping/handling — $1.25 for orders less than $25. For
orders over $25, add 5% of total for shipping and handling. Florida
residents add 5% sales tax.